Motivational QUOTES

A Collection of Quotes for the work or school week.

This book contains 20+ weeks of motivational quotes, note pages and worksheets to guide you through goal setting and personal growth.

Author: Anneke Williams

Table of Contents

- I. Forward
- II. About...The Author
- III. Introduction-How this book can be used
- IV. A Semester of Quotes
  1) WEEK 1-Future/Goal Planning
  2) WEEK 2-Self-Discipline
  3) WEEK 3-Focus
  4) WEEK 4-Character
  5) WEEK 5-Champions
  6) WEEK-6-I will Finish Strong *(Teacher Sample)*
  7) WEEK 7-Dream the Impossible *(Teacher Sample)*
  8) WEEK 8-Either Move or Be Moved
  9) WEEK 9-I will Overcome the Challenge
  10) WEEK 10-Ability is Knowledge in Action
  11) WEEK 11-I will Act Now! Change is Imminent
  12) WEEK 12-There's no Substitute for Hard Work
  13) WEEK 13-I Will Succeed! Step by Step
  14) WEEK 14-We Can't Help Everyone, but Everyone can Help Someone
  15) WEEK 15-A Hero is a Man Who is Afraid to Run Away
  16) WEEK 16-Out of Difficulties Grow Miracles
  17) WEEK 17-Every Day, in Every Way, I Am Getting Better and Better
  18) WEEK 18-<u>Self Series</u>-Self-Control
  19) WEEK 19-<u>Self Series</u>-Discover Self-Improvement, Grow
  20) WEEK 20-<u>Self Series</u>-Building Self-Confidence
- V. African American Leaders-Motivational Quotes
- VI. Hispanic Leaders-Motivational Quotes
- VII. Coaches-Motivational Quotes
- VIII. Presidents-Motivational Quotes
- IX. Appendix-Templates
  - A. Worksheet Samples 1 & 2
  - B. Worksheet Chart Samples 1 & 2
  - C. Spiral Notebook: Directions for daily quotes; in-depth study
- X. Bibliography

I. Forward

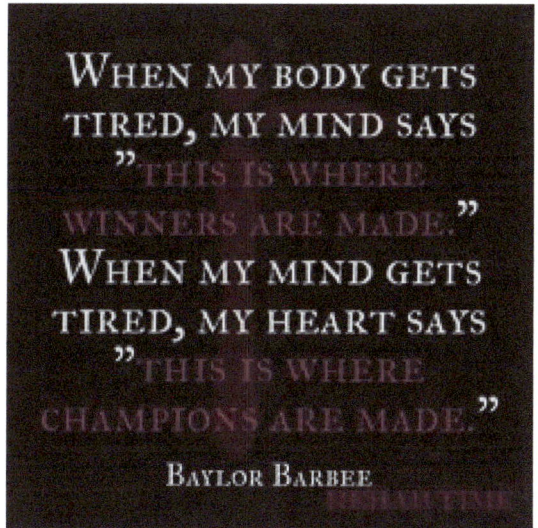

"The things you do for yourself are gone when you are gone, but the things you do for others remain as your legacy." ~ Kalu Kalu

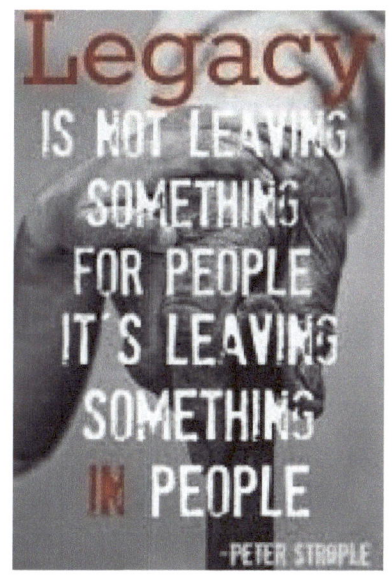

Forward...

The idea for this book was born...

I have always loved finding good quotes. Well before my teaching career started, I would see, hear or find quotes that helped motivate me. I would write them down and keep them in a notebook. I would make some quotes into small posters to hang on my bedroom wall. Later, I would hang these quotes in my classroom or office. I found that my students, and co-workers, like them too, a lot.

Motivational quotes have played a big role in my career. I have used quotes in groups (part of a social skills curriculum) and as writing prompts. I believe that each quote has the potential to be "The One" that sparks a connection with a student; that motivates/inspires them. I have and continue to use them for personal motivation and with my two girls.

By God's hand, I was hired to serve as a Special Education Teacher at a district's DAEP (District's Alternative Education Program). My collection of quotes began to grow even larger as they became an important part of the students' school day. I continue to purposely research quotes at home to add to this collection. I try to focus on motivational quotes that would speak on specific topics; hard work, goal setting, purpose, and so forth. This motivational piece caught on and has been implemented into a social skills building curriculum. My collection now contains 20 weeks' worth of quotes, a semester plus and more. The students really enjoy hearing new quotes each day.

This is also where I met my wonderful husband, David. Meeting him is the main reason I know God's hand is in my life. He has encouraged me to take my love of quotes and my collection to write this book.

I would also like to thank my sis-in-law Chrys. She supported me during the whole process of writing this book. Her excitement for my book re-ignited my passion and helped me finish it. This helped me realize there are more people out there who have a love of quotes and enjoy using them to motivate themselves and others.

II. About…The Author

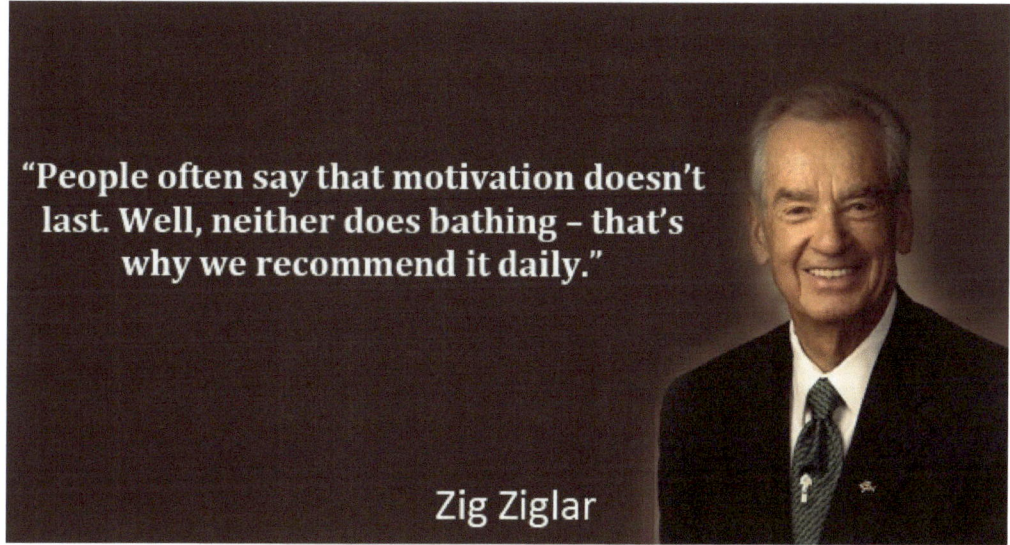

What you get
by achieving your goals
is not as important
as what you become
by achieving your goals.
~Zig Ziglar

Ziglar.com

About the author...

I have been working with children with behavioral and/or emotional disorders for over 25 years in various public school settings; crossing all grade levels with a focus in secondary. My first teaching position was right out of college in a high school self-contained behavior program. You could say I was thrown into the "lion's den," but it was the best learning year I could have ever asked for. It was the foundation that prepared me for the years ahead. The totality of my experience was gained in 10 districts, covering 9 cities in 3 states. This has allowed me to pull the best methods, interventions, and experience from many established programs/schools/mentors. I have overseen several self-contained programs, developed a Social Skills curriculum, and implemented social/mentor groups. I have trained para-professionals (teacher's aides) and teachers with a focus on behavior, classroom management and student interactions. I have also developed home plans for families with children who have an emotional disability/behavior problems. My teaching years also gave me the opportunity to coach various junior and high school sports, serve(d) as a department chair, campus and district discipline committee contributor, and campus/district behavior specialist.

I am currently a special education, 504 and ESL liaison, DTLT (District Technology Leadership Team) member, and campus testing coordinator at a DAEP (District Alternative Education Placement) campus.

I am married with two wonderful girls. My husband David also works in education and has over 25 years' experience in the field of alternative education. Our oldest daughter, Aleathia, is a junior in high school, has a wonderful love and gift for working with horses, art, volleyball and running. Savanna is a freshman in high school and excels in sports and enjoys baking, and any craft/DIY that crosses her path. We "divide and conquer" when it comes to our two beautiful and talented girls. They keep everyone hopping and enjoying life.

I really enjoy working with the at risk population no matter what "label" they may have been given. I wouldn't trade all my years in teaching for anything.

III.   Introduction-How this book can be used

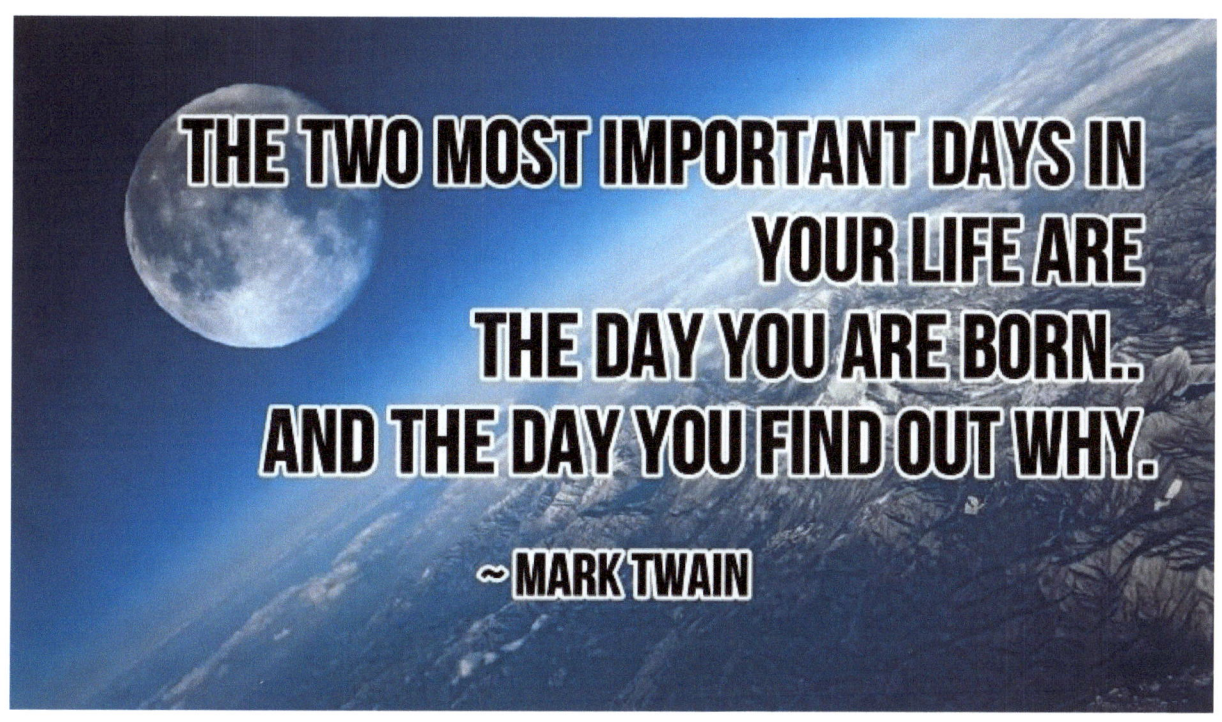

Introduction-How this book can be used...

What started out as a collection has turned into a curriculum. This can be used as a warm-up, piece of or full social skills curriculum, piece of a teen leadership program, or a motivational piece for a campus. This can also be used for personal growth, focusing on goal setting and/or journaling

There are twenty weeks of quotes. This is enough to cover an entire semester. There are templates in the back to choose from to help guide you through. The templates are in worksheet, chart or journal form. Two weeks of examples are included for teachers that include content and language objectives. Over the years, my research moved forward to find more quotes, so I added four extra sections. These sections include motivational quotes from presidents, Hispanic Leaders, African American Leaders and Coaches.

You can incorporate the quotes and the lessons as in-depth as you would like. You can have students copy the quote and discuss it for a quick warm-up. You could implement it to its fullest potential which includes vocabulary, contextual use of words, research on authors, interpretation, acrostics and implementation to personal goal setting. Any of these strategies can also be implemented with the four additional sections described above.

This was developed to find the one or two quotes that would personally speak to an individual. Sometimes all it takes is a special phrase or verse to have a life lesson "click." The intent is that through this curriculum, many lives will be affected and changed for the better.

Good luck, have fun with it...write and/or highlight in this book, feel free to make copies of the templates or follow the spiral directions in your own journal or spiral.

=People often say that motivation doesn't last. Well, neither does bathing—that's why we recommend it daily.

                     Zig Ziglar

=Strength does not come from winning. Your struggles develop your strengths. When you go through hardships and decide not to surrender, that is strength.

        Arnold Schwarzenegger

IV. Semester of Quotes

Monday

WEEK 1: FUTURE, GOAL PLANNING

- ❖ Though no one can go back and make a brand new start, anyone can start from now and make a <u>brand new ending</u>.

    <u>Carl Bard</u>

- ❖ SMART Goals: **S**pecific, **M**easurable, **A**ctions, **R**ealistic, **T**ime-line.

TAKE OVER
-How does the quote relate to the words "take over?"
-How can you apply this quote to your current situation?
-What do the words "take over" mean to you?

KEY WORDS   -brand new ending

ACROSTIC   -CHARACTER
    C*ourage*
    Honest
    Attitude
    R*esponsible*
    Ambition
    Courteous
    Tenacity
    E*tiquette*
    R*espectful*

NOTES:
_____
_____
_____
_____
_____
_____

Tuesday

WEEK 1: FUTURE, GOAL PLANNING

- I will permit no man to narrow and <u>degrade</u> my soul by making me hate him.

- <u>Character</u> is power.

- Character, not <u>circumstances</u>, makes the man.

  <u>Booker T. Washington</u>

- Setting goals is the first step in turning the invisible to the visible.
  <u>Tony Robbins</u>

TAKE OVER — If someone says something that makes me feel uncomfortable how can I handle it without conflict or letting that person take over how the rest of the day goes?

KEY WORDS
- degrade
- circumstances
- tenacity
- character

Define what these words mean to you.

ACROSTIC — POWER

NOTES:
_____
_____
_____
_____
_____
_____
_____

Wednesday

WEEK 1: FUTURE, GOAL PLANNING

- Everyone has a success mechanism and a failure mechanism. The failure mechanism goes off by itself. The success mechanism only goes off with a goal. Every time we write down and talk about a goal we push the button to start the success mechanism.

    Charles 'Tremendous' Jones

- Setting a goal is not the main thing. It is deciding how you will go about achieving it and staying with that plan.

    Tom Landry

TAKE OVER
- What triggers your success mechanism?
- What triggers your failure mechanism?
- How can you apply the success mechanism and failure mechanism to taking over a successful future for YOURSELF??

KEY WORDS   Use each in a positive sentence, aimed at your goal.
- success
- failure
- mechanism
- goal
- setting
- deciding
- achieving
- plan

ACROSTIC   -SUCCESS

NOTES:
___
___
___
___
___
___

Thursday

WEEK 1: FUTURE, GOAL PLANNING

- ❖ <u>Crystallize</u> your goals. Make a plan for <u>achieving</u> them and set yourself a deadline. Then, with <u>supreme</u> <u>confidence</u>, <u>determination</u> and <u>disregard</u> for <u>obstacles</u> and other people's <u>criticisms</u>, carry out your plan.

  <u>Paul Meyer</u>

- ❖ What you get by achieving your goals is not as important as what you <u>become</u> by achieving your goals.

  <u>Zig Ziglar</u>

TAKE OVER
-Today you will develop a Take Over Plan that includes:
-A name for your plan
-Your goal/What you want to accomplish
-A plan/How you are going to accomplish/reach your goal
-A Timeline to accomplish/attain your plan

KEY WORD
- -supreme confidence   -determination
- -disregard   -obstacles
- -criticism

ACROSTIC   -CONFIDENCE

NOTES:
_____
_____
_____
_____
_____
_____
_____

Friday

WEEK 1: FUTURE, GOAL PLANNING

- ❖ Write it down. Written goals have a way of <u>transforming</u> <u>wishes</u> into wants; can't into cans; <u>dreams</u> into plans; and plans into <u>reality</u>. **Don't just think it – ink it!**

<u>Michael Korda</u>

- ❖ The victory of success is half won when one gains the habit of setting and achieving goals.

<u>Og Mandino</u>

- ❖ If you aim at nothing, you will hit it every time.

<u>Zig Ziglar</u>

TAKE OVER — How will the plan you wrote yesterday help you to *Take Over* a successful future for yourself.

KEY WORDS
- transform
- reality *vs.* dreams/wishes
- obstacles
- criticism

ACROSTIC — INK IT

NOTES:

_____
_____
_____
_____
_____
_____

Monday

WEEK 2: SELF-DISCIPLINE

- ❖ The difference between <u>perseverance</u> and <u>obstinacy</u> is that one comes from a strong <u>will</u>, and the other a strong won't.

    <u>Henry Ward Beecher</u>

- ❖ <u>Self-Respect</u> is the root of discipline: The sense of <u>dignity</u> grows with the ability to say no to oneself.

    <u>Abraham Joshua Heschel</u>

TAKE OVER -What will you do when your mind tells you I can do no more, but deep down in your heart you know you can?

KEY WORDS
-persevere -self-respect
-obstinacy -dignity
-will

ACROSTIC: -*Your name OR title of your future (dream) job*

NOTES:

_____
_____
_____
_____
_____
_____
_____

Tuesday

WEEK 2: SELF-DISCIPLINE

- Hold yourself <u>responsible</u> for a higher <u>standard</u> than anybody else <u>expects</u> of you. Never excuse yourself. Never pity yourself. Be a hard <u>master</u> to yourself – and be <u>lenient</u> to everybody else.

<u>Henry Ward Beecher</u>

- <u>Self-discipline</u> is the ability to make yourself do what you should do, when you should do it, whether you feel like it or not.

<u>Elbert Hubbard</u>

TAKE OVER -Solve – a farmer is taking a fox, a chicken, and a bag of grain home. To get there he must cross a river, but he can only take one item at a time. How can the farmer cross the river without any of his possessions being eaten?

KEY WORDS
- responsible
- standard
- expect (expectations)
- Master
- Lenient

ACROSTIC -STANDARD

NOTES:
_____
_____
_____
_____
_____
_____
_____

Wednesday

WEEK 2: SELF-DISCIPLINE

❖ Our <u>ultimate</u> <u>freedom</u> is the <u>right</u> and <u>power</u> to decide how anybody or anything outside ourselves will <u>affect</u> us.

<u>Stephen Covey</u>

❖ The ability to <u>discipline</u> yourself, to <u>delay gratification</u> in the short term in order to enjoy greater rewards in the long term, is the <u>indispensable</u> prerequisite for <u>success</u>.

<u>Maxwell Maltz</u>

TAKE OVER
-Solve the following:
-A farmer had 9 sheep. All but 7 died. How many does he have left?
-At a family get together there was a son, daughter, mom, dad, aunt, uncle, niece, nephew and a cousin. However, only 4 people were present. How is this possible?

KEY WORDS
- ultimate freedom
- right
- affect
- power
- discipline
- delay gratification
- indispensable
- success

ACROSTIC   -FREEDOM

NOTES:
_____
_____
_____
_____
_____
_____

Thursday

WEEK 2: SELF-DISCIPLINE

❖ Class is an <u>aura</u> of <u>confidence</u> that is being sure without being cocky. Class has nothing to do with money. Class never runs scared. It is <u>self-discipline</u> and <u>self-knowledge</u>. It's the <u>sure footedness</u> that comes with having proved you can meet life.

<u>Ann Landers</u>

❖ What it lies in our <u>power</u> to do, it lies in our <u>power</u> not to do.

<u>Aristotle</u>

TAKE OVER -How does having class align with having self-discipline?
-What's the difference between someone who has class and someone who does not?

KEY WORDS -aura   -confidence
-self-discipline   -self-knowledge
-sure footedness   -power

ACROSTIC -CONFIDENCE

NOTES:
_____
_____
_____
_____
_____
_____
_____

Friday

WEEK 2: SELF-DISCIPLINE

- ❖ If it turns out that my best wasn't good enough, at least I won't look back and say that I was <u>afraid</u> to try; failure makes me work even harder.

  <u>Michael Jordan</u>

- ❖ Failure is only the opportunity to begin again more intelligently.

  <u>Henry Ford</u>

TAKE OVER
- How can knowing your fear make you stronger, more successful?
- What is your fear?

KEY WORDS
- Afraid   (to succeed?)   (to fail?)   (of the unknown?)
- Describe a time when you were afraid and if you overcame your fear. How did you overcome? If not, what did you learn from the failure?

ACROSTIC   -OVERCOME

NOTES:

_____
_____
_____
_____
_____
_____
_____

Monday

WEEK 3: FOCUS

- ❖ If you <u>focus</u> on <u>results</u>, you will never change. If you focus on <u>change</u>, you will get results.

  <u>Jack Dixon</u>

- ❖ Focus on the positive, <u>defend</u> your <u>mind</u> against the negative, and <u>expect victory</u>.

  <u>Billy Cox</u>

TAKE OVER
- What is your focus in life and why?
- What results do you hope to achieve in 5 years, 10 years?

KEY WORDS
- focus
- change
- results
- defend
- mind
- expect victory

ACROSTIC
- FOCUS

NOTES:
_____
_____
_____
_____
_____
_____

Tuesday

WEEK 3: FOCUS

❖ Most people have no idea of the giant <u>capacity</u> we can immediately <u>command</u> when we focus all of our <u>resources</u> on mastering a single area of our lives.

<u>Anthony Robbins</u>

❖ I fear not the man who has practiced 10,000 kicks once, but I fear the man who has practiced one kick 10,000 times.

<u>Bruce Lee</u>

TAKE OVER   -What are "all" the resources you have to support you?

KEY WORDS   -focus
-capacity
-command
-resources

ACROSTIC   -CAPACITY

NOTES:
_____
_____
_____
_____
_____
_____
_____

Wednesday

WEEK 3: FOCUS

- ❖ A man of <u>sense</u> is never discouraged by difficulties; he redoubles his <u>industry</u> and his <u>diligence</u>, he <u>perseveres</u> and <u>infallibly</u> <u>prevails</u> at last.

   <u>Lord Chesterfield</u>

- ❖ <u>Concentrate</u> all your <u>thoughts</u> upon the <u>work</u> at hand. The sun's rays do not burn until brought to <u>a focus</u>.

   <u>Alexander Graham Bell</u>

- ❖ Focus like a laser, not a flashlight.

   <u>Michael Jordan</u>

TAKE OVER — Write Lord Chesterfield's quote in your own words.

KEY WORDS
- -sense
- -industry
- -diligence
- -prevails
- -infallibly
- -perseveres
- -work
- -a focus
- -concentrate

ACROSTIC — DILIGENCE

NOTES:
_____
_____
_____
_____
_____
_____

Thursday

WEEK 3: FOCUS

- ❖ I never did anything by accident, nor did any of my inventions come by accident; they came by <u>work</u>.

    Thomas Edison

- ❖ The successful man is the average man, <u>focused</u>.

    Ralph Waldo Emerson

- ❖ If you chase two rabbits, both will escape.

    Author unknown

TAKE OVER — Combine the above quotes into one…what do they say to you?

KEY WORDS — explain how focus "fits" into the two quotes that do NOT contain the word.
-work

ACROSTIC WORK

NOTES:
_____
_____
_____
_____
_____
_____

Friday

WEEK 3: FOCUS

- ❖ I <u>will</u> beat her. I will <u>train</u> harder. I will eat cleaner. I know her weaknesses. I know her strengths. I've lost to her before, but not this time. She is going down. I have the <u>advantage</u> because I know her well. She is <u>the old me</u>.

<u>Bonnie Pfiester</u>

- ❖ The secret of <u>change</u> is to <u>focus</u> all your <u>energy</u>, not on fighting the old, but on <u>building the new</u>.

<u>Socrates</u>

TAKE OVER -The only person you truly compete against is yourself. Knowing this and using these quotes, describe what you are going to do next to be a better, stronger, more confident you.

KEY WORDS
- -will
- -train
- -advantage
- -the old me

- -focus
- -change
- -energy
- -building the new

ACROSTIC YOUR FULL NAME

NOTES:
_____
_____
_____
_____
_____
_____

Monday

WEEK 4: CHARACTER

❖ No change of <u>circumstance</u> can repair a <u>defect</u> of character.

<u>Ralph Waldo Emmerson</u>

❖ Weakness of <u>attitude</u> becomes weakness of <u>character</u>.

<u>Albert Einstein</u>

❖ When the character of a man is not clear to you, look at his <u>friends</u>.
<u>Chinese Proverb</u>

TAKE OVER — When people speak negatively about you, what are some things you have learned in this book so far, or life, that will help you show that they are wrong?

KEY WORDS
- circumstance
- attitude
- friends
- defect
- character

ACROSTIC — CHARACTER (Again)

NOTES:
_____
_____
_____
_____
_____
_____

Tuesday

WEEK 4: CHARACTER

❖ <u>Character</u> cannot be developed in ease and quiet. Only through experiences of <u>trial and suffering</u> can the soul be strengthened, vision cleared, <u>ambition</u> <u>inspired</u> and success achieved.

<u>Helen Keller</u>

❖ Being the richest man in the cemetery doesn't matter to me. Going to bed at night saying we've done something wonderful, that's what matters to me.

<u>Steve Jobs</u>

TAKE OVER   -How do you develop positive character?
                            -What does it take to keep positive character for a lifetime?

KEY WORDS   -character
                             -trial and suffering
                             -ambition   -inspired
                             -wonderful

ACROSTIC   -AMBITION

NOTES:
_____
_____
_____
_____
_____
_____
_____

Wednesday

WEEK 4: CHARACTER

❖ Character is always lost when a high ideal is sacrificed on the altar of conformity and popularity.

Unknown Author

❖ Character is the result of two things: Mental attitude and the way we spend our time.

Elbert Hubbard

❖ Character, not circumstance, makes the person.

Booker T. Washington

TAKE OVER — Although many teachers thought little of me, I turned out to be a genius who changed the world. I suppose I proved that all things are relative. Who am I?

KEY WORDS
- character
- altar
- mental attitude
- high ideal
- conformity

ACROSTIC — HIGH IDEAL

NOTES:
_____
_____
_____
_____
_____
_____

Thursday

WEEK 4: CHARACTER

- Watch your thoughts; they become words. Watch your words; they become actions. Watch your actions; they become habit. Watch your habits; they become <u>character</u>. Watch your <u>character</u>; it becomes your <u>destiny</u>.

  <u>Frank outlaw</u>

- Character is like a tree and reputation like a shadow. The shadow is what we think of it; the tree is the real thing.

  <u>Abraham Lincoln</u>

TAKE OVER
-Match this quote to something in your life (something you thought, then said, then did. etc.)
-If you cannot match it, put it in place for your goal. (I need to think _____, and say _____, and do _____, etc.)

KEY WORDS
-destiny
-character

ACROSTIC
-DESTINY

NOTES:
_____
_____
_____
_____
_____
_____

Friday

WEEK 4: CHARACTER

- No <u>pain</u>, no <u>palm</u>; no <u>thorns</u>, no <u>throne</u>; no <u>gall</u>, no <u>glory</u>; no <u>cross</u>, no <u>crown</u>.

    <u>William Penn</u>

- <u>Character</u> consists of what you do on the third and fourth tries.

    <u>James A. Michener</u>

- Character, like a photograph, develops in darkness.

    <u>Yousuf Karsh</u>

TAKE OVER — Re-write William Penn's quote substituting a synonym for each word underlined (double and single). YOUR rewrite should reflect YOUR personal goal YOU are working towards.

KEY WORDS
- palm
- thorns   (double underlined)
- throne
- gall

ACROSTIC — TAKE-OVER

NOTES:

_____
_____
_____
_____
_____
_____

Monday

WEEK 5: CHAMPIONS

- <u>Champions</u> aren't made in gyms. <u>Champions</u> are made from something they have deep inside them: A <u>desire</u>, a dream, a <u>vision</u>. They have to have <u>late minute stamina</u>, they have to be a little faster, they have to have the skill and the <u>will</u>. But the will must be stronger than the skill.

<u>Muhammad Ali</u>

- You are a champion! You are not a champ because you are the strongest or the best. You are a champion because you <u>refuse to give up</u>.

<u>Bonnie Pfiester</u>

TAKE OVER — Explain how you will demonstrate living the life of a champion.

KEY WORDS
- champion   -will   -stamina
- desire/vision — how do these two terms relate
- late minute   -refuse to give up

ACROSTIC — CHAMPIONS

NOTES:
_____
_____
_____
_____
_____
_____
_____

Tuesday

WEEK 5: CHAMPIONS

- Every <u>champion</u> was a <u>contender</u> that <u>refused</u> to give up.

  <u>Rocky Balboa</u>

- I don't count my sit ups—I only start counting when it starts hurting. That is when I start counting, because then it <u>really counts</u>. That's what makes you a <u>champion</u>.

  <u>Muhammad Ali</u>

- To be a champ, you must <u>believe</u> in yourself when no one else will.

  <u>Sugar Ray Robinson</u>

TAKE OVER — What is a champion to you? Give of an example of a champion that is not sports related.

KEY WORDS
- champion
- refused
- really counts
- contender
- believe

ACROSTIC — CHAMPION

NOTES:

_____
_____
_____
_____
_____
_____

Wednesday

WEEK 5: CHAMPIONS

- Perfection is not attainable. But if we chase perfection, we can catch excellence.

  Vince Lombardi

- To become a champion requires a good mental attitude toward preparation. You have to accept the most tedious task with pleasure.

  Bruce Lee

TAKE OVER -Write five things you can do to live the life style of a champion. How will you begin applying these five things to your life.

KEY WORDS
- perfection
- excellence
- mental attitude
- preparation
- tedious

ACROSTIC -PREPARATION

NOTES:
_____
_____
_____
_____
_____
_____

Thursday

WEEK 5: CHAMPIONS

- ❖ I am here for a <u>purpose</u> and that purpose is to <u>grow</u> into a <u>mountain</u>, not to shrink to a grain of sand. Henceforth I will apply ALL my <u>efforts</u> to become the highest mountain of all and I will <u>strain</u> my <u>potential</u> until it cries for mercy.

<u>Og Mandino</u>

- ❖ The difference between try and <u>triumph</u> is a little UMPH!

<u>Marvin Philips</u>

TAKE OVER   -Describe the process of growing from a grain of sand into a mountain.

KEY WORDS
- -purpose
- -mountain
- -strain
- -triumph
- -grow
- -efforts
- -potential

ACROSTIC   -TRIUMPH

NOTES:
_____
_____
_____
_____
_____
_____
_____

Friday

WEEK 5: CHAMPIONS

- ❖ The harder the <u>conflict</u>, the more <u>glorious</u> the <u>triumph</u>. What we obtain too cheaply, we <u>esteem</u> too lightly; 'Tis dearness only that gives everything its value.

<u>Thomas Paine</u>

- ❖ It's hard to beat a person who <u>never gives up</u>.

<u>Babe Ruth</u>

TAKE OVER — Explain how you are going to live the lifestyle of a champion, plan it out, use the key word from this week.

KEY WORDS
- conflict
- triumph
- never gives up
- glorious
- esteem

ACROSTIC — GLORIOUS

NOTES:
_____
_____
_____
_____
_____
_____
_____

IV. Teacher Samples-Weeks 6 & 7

"I have been given eyes to see and a mind to think and now I know a great secret of life for I perceive, at last, that all my problems, discouragements, and heartaches are, in truth, great opportunities in disguise"
~Og Mandino

Monday

WEEK 6: I WILL Finish Strong

❖ Forget about likes and dislikes. They are of no <u>consequence</u>. Just do what must be done. This may not be happiness but it is <u>greatness</u>.

<u>George Bernard Shaw</u>

The Tortoise and the Hare
an Aesop Fable

One day a hare was bragging about how fast he could run. He bragged and bragged and even laughed at the tortoise, who was so slow. The tortoise stretched out his long neck and challenged the hare to a race, which, of course, made the hare laugh.

"My, my, what a joke!" thought the hare. "A race, indeed, a race." Oh! What fun! My, my! A race, of course, Mr. Tortoise, we shall race!" said the hare.

The forest animals met and mapped out the course. The race begun, and the hare, being such a swift runner, soon left the tortoise far behind. About halfway through the course, it occurred to the hare that he had plenty of time to beat the slow trodden tortoise.

"Oh, my!" thought the hare, "I have plenty of time to play in the meadow here." And so he did. After the hare finished playing, he decided that he had time to take a little nap. "I have plenty of time to beat that tortoise," he thought. And he cuddle up against a tree and dozed. The tortoise, in the meantime, continued to plod on, albeit, it ever so slowly. He never stopped, but took one good step after another.

The hare finally woke from his nap. "Time to get going," he thought. And off he went faster than he had ever run before! He dashed as quickly as anyone ever could up to the finish line, where he met the tortoise, who was patiently awaiting his arrival.

Content Objective (CO): TSWBAT gain a clear understanding of what "I will finish strong" means.

Language Objective (LO): TLW use the two key words to tell how they will finish strong in life.

TAKE OVER	-How did the tortoise beat the hare in the race? -When it comes to finishing strong in life, which one are you, the tortoise or the hare? Why?
KEY WORDS	-greatness -consequence
ACROSTIC	-GREATNESS

Tuesday

WEEK 6: I WILL Finish Strong

- LEGACY-You need not worry about how you will be remembered. Instead, focus on living a life of <u>character</u>, <u>conviction</u>, and <u>compassion</u> and your legacy will never be forgotten.

  <u>Dr. Robyn Silverman</u>

- How you use the opportunities you are given to affect the world around you will determine the <u>legacy</u> you leave behind.

  <u>Tony Dungy</u>

Content Objective (CO): TSWBAT tell "His-Story" of how finishing strong will lead to greatness in their lives.

Language Objective (LO): TLW use the keyword greatness to describe their future.

TAKE OVER
-Write down today's date five years from now.
-Write down five things people will say about your history five years from now.

KEY WORDS
-legacy
-character
-compassion
-conviction

ACROSTIC -LEGACY

NOTES:
_____
_____
_____
_____
_____
_____

Wednesday

WEEK 6: I WILL Finish Strong

- ❖ The <u>ultimate</u> <u>measure</u> of a man is not where he stands in moments of comfort and <u>convenience</u>, but where he stands at times of <u>challenge</u> and <u>controversy</u>.

<u>Martin Luther King Jr.</u>

- ❖ Regardless of what came <u>before</u> or of what has <u>yet to come</u>, what matters most right <u>now</u> is how I <u>choose</u> to respond to the challenge before me. Will I lie down or will I fight? The choice is mine and I choose to <u>Finish Strong</u>!

<u>Dan Green</u>

Content Objective (CO): TSWBAT evaluate their ability to finish strong when faced with overcoming adversity and life challenging situations.

Language Objective (LO): TLW use the key words ultimate measure, convenience, challenge, and controversy to explain how they will finish strong in life.

TAKE OVER — What is standing in your way? What do you have to overcome? Is it your past, present, future fear? Write it down and plan to finish strong.

KEY WORDS
- ultimate measure
- controversy
- now
- convenience
- before
- choose
- challenge
- yet to come
- finish strong

ACROSTIC -FINISH STRONG

NOTES:
_____
_____
_____
_____

Thursday

WEEK 6: I WILL Finish Strong

- ❖ A constant <u>struggle</u>, a <u>ceaseless</u> battle to bring success from <u>inhospitable</u> surroundings, is the price of all great <u>achievements</u>.

    <u>Orison Swett Marden</u>

- ❖ Here is a test to find whether your mission on earth is <u>finished</u>: If you are alive, it isn't.

    <u>Richard Bach</u>

Content Objective (CO): TSWBAT understand that there may be many battles to win in order to finish strong.

Language Objective (LO): TLW use the four key words to describe a personal battle they overcame that ended with successful results.

TAKE OVER — Using the key words write 1-2 paragraphs about one or more battles you foresee in order for you to finish strong.

KEY WORDS
- struggle
- inhospitable
- achievements
- ceaseless
- finished

ACROSTIC — STRUGGLE

NOTES:

_____
_____
_____
_____
_____
_____

Friday

WEEK 6: I WILL Finish Strong

- ❖ No man is truly great who is great only in his lifetime. The test of <u>greatness</u> is the page of history.

<u>William Hazlitt</u>

- ❖ If I fail, I <u>try again</u>, <u>and again</u>, <u>and again</u>. If you fail are you going to try again? The <u>human spirit</u> can handle much worse than we realize. It matters <u>HOW</u> **you** are going to <u>finish</u>. Are you going to <u>finish strong</u>?

<u>Nick Vujicic</u>

Content Objective (CO): TSWBAT find their will to finish strong in life.

Language Objective (LO): Create a crossword puzzle using five keywords. The learners will also write sentences to support their crossword puzzles.

TAKE OVER	-Explain in your own words what today's quotes mean to you. How can it affect the way you live? What do you know about Nic?
KEY WORDS	-struggle -try again -how -finish -human spirit
ACROSTIC	-HUMAN SPIRIT

NOTES:

_____
_____
_____
_____

Monday

WEEK 7: DREAM THE IMPOSSIBLE

❖ So many of our <u>dreams</u> at first seem <u>impossible</u>, then they seem <u>improbable</u>, and then when we <u>summon</u> the will, they soon become <u>inevitable</u>.

<u>Christopher Reeve</u>

Content Objective (CO): TSWBAT gain a clear understanding of how having a positive mindset can help them, not only dream, but live the impossible.

Language Objective (LO): TLW identify implicit ideas and information written in Reeves' quote. TLW use the five keywords to describe how you will live your dream.

TAKE OVER -List five things you must do to dream and live what seems impossible and why.

KEY WORDS
-dream
-impossible
-improbable
-summon
-inevitable

ACROSTIC -DREAM

NOTES:
_____
_____
_____
_____
_____
_____
_____

Tuesday

WEEK 7: DREAM THE IMPOSSIBLE

- ❖ You have all the reason in the world to achieve your <u>grandest</u> dreams. Imagination plus <u>innovation</u> equals <u>realization</u>.

  <u>Denis Waitley</u>

- ❖ Hold fast to <u>dreams</u>, for if dreams die, life is like a broken winged bird that cannot fly.
  <u>Langston Hughes</u>

Content Objective (CO): TSWBAT realize dreams are not impossible if they believe.

Language Objective (LO): TLW identify words and phrases written in Waitley's and Hughes' quotes that support dreaming and living the impossible.

TAKE OVER	- Write five reasons why we should write positive dreams down on paper. -Next write down three different ways to accomplish your positive identified dream.
KEY WORDS	-grandest -innovation -realization -dreams -imagination (as in dreams not pretending)
ACROSTIC	-REALIZATION

NOTES:

_____
_____
_____
_____

Wednesday

WEEK 7: DREAM THE IMPOSSIBLE

❖ I will! I am! I can! I will <u>actualize my dream</u>. I will <u>press ahead</u>. I will <u>settle down</u> and <u>see it through</u>. I will <u>solve problems</u>. I will <u>pay the price</u>. I will never walk away from my dream until I see my dream walk away: Alert! Alive! Achieved!

<u>Robert Schuller</u>

Content Objective (CO): TSWBAT use Schuller's quote to "refresh" (adjust) their current dream (goal).

Language Objective (LO): TLW write a word for each key word phrase listed, then use these words to write out their current dream (goal).

TAKE OVER
- You are in a race and take over the person who is in second place. What is your current position now?
- Re-write your dream and break down the steps into smaller mini goals. Explain how breaking your goal into steps helps.

KEY WORD
- actualize my dream
- settle down
- solve problems
- press ahead
- see it through
- pay the price

ACROSTIC -BELIEVE

NOTES:
_____
_____
_____
_____
_____
_____

Thursday

WEEK 7: DREAM THE IMPOSSIBLE

- ❖ The problems of this world cannot possibly be solved by <u>skeptics</u> or <u>cynics</u> whose <u>horizons</u> are <u>limited</u> by the <u>obvious realities</u>. We need men who can dream of things that never were.

    <u>John F. Kennedy</u>

- ❖ We've got to have a dream if we are going to make a dream come true.

    <u>Denis Waitley</u>

Content Objective (CO): TSWBAT describe how to move past skeptics and cynics to reach their dream.

Language Objective (LO): TLW define the 5 key words and use them appropriately to complete the takeover.

TAKE OVER	-Write 3-5 things skeptics or cynics have said to you concerning reaching your dream. -Explain how you will now respond to those statements to demonstrate that you WILL reach your impossible dream.
KEY WORDS	-skeptics -cynics -horizons -limited -obvious realities
ACROSTIC	-IMPOSSIBLE

NOTES:
_____
_____
_____
_____

Friday

WEEK 7: DREAM THE IMPOSSIBLE

❖ You control your future, your destiny. <u>What you think about comes about</u>. By <u>recording</u> your <u>dreams</u> and <u>goals</u> on paper, you <u>set in motion</u> the <u>process</u> of <u>becoming</u> the person you most want to be. <u>Put your future in good hands – your own</u>.

<u>Mark Victor Hansen</u>

Content Objective (CO): TSWBAT understand that consistent positive thinking is the first step to the realization of their dreams; by developing a positive statement they can repeat daily.

Language Objective (LO): TLW solve both brain teasers in the Take Over.

TAKE OVER -Explain what Mark means by "What you think about comes about." What do you think about? How can you change your thinking to change what "comes about?"

KEY WORDS   -recording   -dreams
                  -goals   -set in motion
                  -process   -becoming
                  -What you think about comes about.
                  -Put your future in good hands-your own.

ACROSTIC   -POSITIVE THINKING

NOTES:
_____
_____
_____
_____
_____

Monday

WEEK 8: EITHER MOVE OR BE MOVED (Colin Powell)

- ❖ You were born to win, but to be a <u>winner</u> you must <u>plan</u> to win, <u>prepare</u> to win, and <u>expect</u> to win.

  <u>Zig Ziglar</u>

- ❖ The <u>self</u> is not something <u>ready-made</u>, but something in <u>continuous formation</u> through <u>choice of action</u>.

  <u>John Dewey</u>

TAKE OVER — So, write your plan, yes, again. State any progress you have made and set new stepping stone goals if necessary.

KEY WORDS
- winner
- prepare
- self
- continuous formation
- choice of action
- plan
- expect
- ready-made

ACROSTIC — WINNER

NOTES:
_____
_____
_____
_____
_____
_____
_____

Tuesday

WEEK 8: EITHER MOVE OR BE MOVED (Colin Powell)

- ❖ The <u>superior man</u> acts before he speaks, and afterwards speaks <u>according</u> to his actions.

    <u>Confucius</u>

- ❖ It was <u>character</u> that got us out of bed, <u>commitment</u> that moved us into <u>action</u> and <u>discipline</u> that enabled us to <u>follow through</u>.

    <u>Zig Ziglar</u>

TAKE OVER -If you say it, follow through. If you don't plan to follow through, don't say it. Next step, you say it…write it and then act on it.

KEY WORDS
- superior man
- character
- action
- discipline
- follow through
- according
- commitment

ACROSTIC -ACTION

NOTES:
_____
_____
_____
_____
_____
_____
_____

Wednesday

WEEK 8: EITHER MOVE OR BE MOVED (Colin Powell)

- ❖ Waiting is a trap. There will always be reason to wait. The truth is, there are only two things in life, <u>reasons</u> and <u>results</u>, and reasons simply don't count.

    Dr. Robert Anthony

TAKE OVER
-Explain in 3+ sentences what positive impact this week's title can make, "Either Move or Be Moved."
-Develop an inspirational quote of your own using the meaning of Colin Powell and Dr. Anthony's quotes.

KEY WORDS
-reasons
-results

ACROSTIC
-MOVE

NOTES:
_____
_____
_____
_____
_____
_____
_____

Thursday

WEEK 8: EITHER MOVE OR BE MOVED (Colin Powell)

- ❖ Plan your <u>progress</u> carefully; hour-by hour, day-by day, month-by month. <u>Organized</u> activity and <u>maintained</u> <u>enthusiasm</u> are the <u>wellsprings</u> of your <u>power</u>.

Paul J. Meyer

TAKE OVER   -Make or get a goal calendar. Write your goal in today's date, then day-by-day or week-by-week set smaller goals aimed at your main goal. Also chart any and all progress you make each day.

KEY WORDS
- progress
- organized
- maintained
- enthusiasm
- wellsprings
- power

ACROSTIC   -POWER

NOTES:
_____
_____
_____
_____
_____
_____
_____

Friday

WEEK 8: EITHER MOVE OR BE MOVED (Colin Powell)

❖ The people who get on in this world are the people who <u>get up</u> and look for the <u>circumstances</u> they want and, if they can't find them, <u>make them</u>.

<u>George Bernard Shaw</u>

TAKE OVER -You are not your circumstance. You are your actions. Act now.

KEY WORDS
-get up
-circumstances
-make them

ACROSTIC -GET UP

NOTES:
_____
_____
_____
_____
_____
_____
_____

IV. Quotes Continued

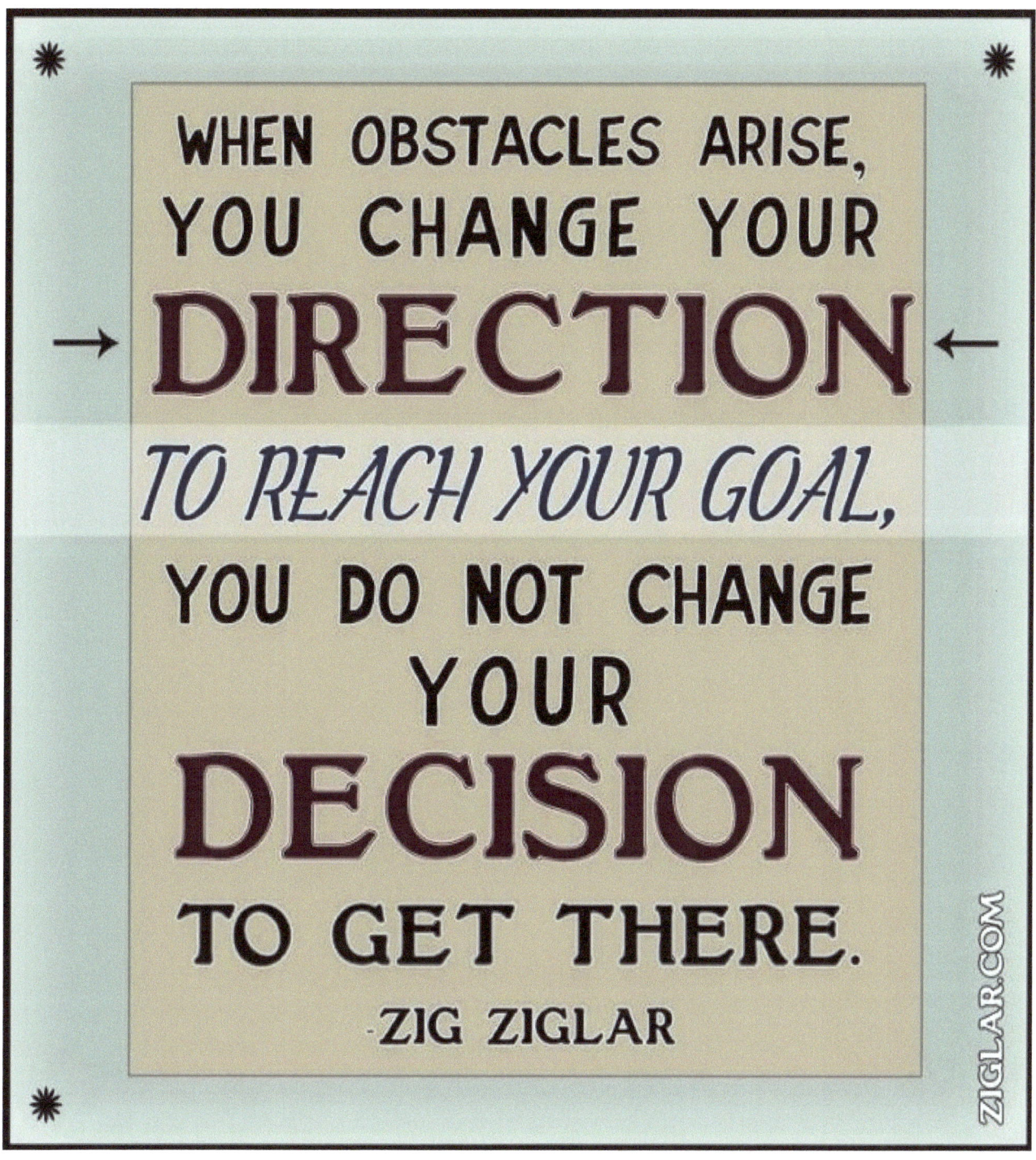

Monday

WEEK 9: I WILL OVERCOME THE CHALLENGE!

- ❖ <u>Challenges</u> are what make life interesting; <u>overcoming</u> them is what makes life meaningful.

    <u>Joshua J. Marine</u>

- ❖ The gem cannot be polished without <u>friction</u>, nor man perfected without <u>trials</u>.

    <u>Chinese Proverb</u>

TAKE OVER   -write five synonyms for challenge and overcome
-compare and contrast the words friction and trial using a double bubble.

Share

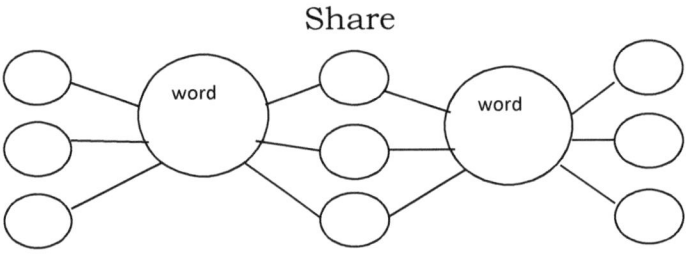

KEY WORDS   -challenges
-overcoming
-friction
-trials

ACROSTIC   -CHALLENGE

NOTES:
_____
_____
_____
_____
_____

Tuesday

WEEK 9: I WILL OVERCOME THE CHALLENGE!

- ❖ You're alive. Do something. The <u>directive</u> in life, the <u>moral imperative</u> was so <u>uncomplicated</u>. It could be expressed in single words, not complete sentences. It sounded like this: <u>Look</u>. <u>Listen</u>. <u>Choose</u>. <u>Act</u>.

    <u>Barbara Hall</u>

- ❖ Don't be afraid your life will end; be afraid that it will never begin.

    <u>Grace Hansen</u>

KEY WORDS
-do something
-moral imperative
-look, listen, choose, act

TAKE OVER
-Update your goal calendar. Add in your statement that you can repeat/think about throughout the day. Think. Write. Do. Continue.

ACROSTIC
-IMPERATIVE

NOTES:
_____
_____
_____
_____
_____
_____
_____

Wednesday

WEEK 9: I WILL OVERCOME THE CHALLENGE!

❖ Never be afraid to do something new. Remember, <u>amateurs</u> built the ark, <u>professionals</u> built the titanic.

<u>Unknown Author</u>

❖ Accept <u>challenges</u>, so that you may feel the <u>exhilaration</u> of <u>victory</u>.

<u>George Patton</u>

TAKE OVER — Part of growth is taking on new tasks. What is something that you have always wanted to do, but have not; volunteer, learn a new skill, be the first to apologize? Make up your mind and GO FOR IT!!

KEY WORDS
- amateurs
- professionals
- challenges
- exhilaration
- victory

ACROSTIC — EXHILARATION

NOTES:
_____
_____
_____
_____
_____
_____

Thursday

WEEK 9: I WILL OVERCOME THE CHALLENGE!

- Twenty years from now you will be more disappointed by the things you didn't do than by the ones you did do. So <u>throw off the bowlines</u>. <u>Sail away from the safe harbor</u>. <u>Catch the trade winds in your sails</u>. <u>Explore</u>. <u>Dream</u>. <u>Discover</u>.

  <u>Mark Twain</u>

- Difficulties are meant to <u>rouse</u>, not <u>discourage</u>. The <u>human spirit</u> is to grow strong by <u>conflict</u>.

  <u>William Ellery Channing</u>

TAKE OVER
- Name 5 things you would like to do in life that you have not done yet.
- Next, tell why you want to do the identified 5 things.
- In what year will you accomplish each?

KEY WORDS
- throw off the bowlines
- sail away from the safe harbor
- catch the trade winds in your sails
- explore
- dream
- discover

ACROSTIC -DISCOVER

NOTES:
_____
_____
_____
_____
_____

Friday

WEEK 9: I WILL OVERCOME THE CHALLENGE!

- ❖ Only those who <u>risk</u> going too far can possibly find out how far one can go.

    <u>T. S. Elliot</u>

- ❖ It's lack of faith that makes people afraid of <u>meeting challenges</u>, and I <u>believe in myself</u>.

    <u>Muhammad Ali</u>

TAKE OVER — What are you afraid of? Identify the true risk, realize the true possibilities, results and move forward. Are you willing to meet the challenge? Write it down!

KEY WORDS
- risk
- meeting challenges
- believe in myself

ACROSTIC — MEET THE CHALLENGE

NOTES:
_____
_____
_____
_____
_____
_____

Monday

WEEK 10: ABILITY IS KNOWLEDGE IN ACTION

❖ Life is not about how hard <u>you can hit</u>. It's about how hard you can <u>get hit</u> and keep <u>moving forward</u>. It's about how much <u>you can take</u> and keep moving forward. It's how winning is done.

<u>Rocky Balboa</u>

TAKE OVER -Explain in your own words what Rocky's quote is saying and apply it to a scenario in your life.

KEY WORDS -you can hit
-get hit
-moving forward
-you can take

ACROSTIC -MOVE FORWARD

NOTES:
___
___
___
___
___
___
___

Tuesday

WEEK 10: ABILITY IS KNOWLEDGE IN ACTION

- ❖ <u>Action</u> is the real measure of <u>intelligence</u>.

    <u>Napoleon Hill</u>

- ❖ <u>Intelligence</u> is not to make no mistakes, but quickly to see how to make them good.

    <u>Elbert Hubbard</u>

- ❖ The great end of life is not <u>knowledge</u> but <u>action</u>.

    <u>Thomas Henry Huxley</u>

TAKE OVER — What are five things you need to accomplish to be considered a man or woman of action and why?

KEY WORDS
- action
- intelligence
- knowledge

Is there a difference? Explain.

ACROSTIC — INTELLIGENCE

NOTES:

_____
_____
_____
_____
_____
_____
_____

Wednesday

WEEK 10: ABILITY IS KNOWLEDGE IN ACTION

- ❖ The real contest is always between what you've done and what you're <u>capable</u> of doing. You measure yourself against yourself and nobody else.

    <u>Geoffrey Gaberino</u>

- ❖ No amount of <u>ability</u> is of the slightest <u>avail</u> without <u>honor</u>.

    <u>Andrew Carnegie</u>

TAKE OVER -Describe a time when you think you did not have any more to give, but you did, you finished, you completed, you succeded. How did you do it? Where did you pull from?

KEY WORDS -capable
-ability
-avail
-honor

ACROSTIC -CAPABLE

NOTES:
_____
_____
_____
_____
_____
_____
_____

Thursday

WEEK 10: ABILITY IS KNOWLEDGE IN ACTION

- ❖ The world cares very little about what a man or woman knows; it is what a man or woman is <u>able</u> to do.

    <u>Booker T. Washington</u>

- ❖ Put yourself in a <u>state of mind</u> where you say to yourself, "Here is an <u>opportunity</u> for me to <u>celebrate</u> like never before, <u>my own power</u>, <u>my own ability</u> to get myself to do whatever is necessary."

    <u>Tony Robbins</u>

TAKE OVER   -You have the will, you have the power, you have the knowledge, you have the ability...what are you going to do now? Write it out.

KEY WORDS   -able
-state of mind
-opportunity
-celebrate
-my own power
-my own ability

ACROSTIC   -KNOWLEDGE

NOTES:
_____
_____
_____
_____
_____
_____

Friday

WEK 10: ABILITY IS KNOWLEDGE IN ACTION

- ❖ The beginning of <u>knowledge</u> is the <u>discovery</u> of something we do not understand.

    <u>Frank Herbert</u>

- ❖ <u>Knowledge</u> is the <u>eye of desire</u> and can become the <u>pilot of the soul</u>.

    <u>Will Durant</u>

- ❖ Your <u>vision</u> will become clear only when you look into your heart. <u>Who looks outside, dreams. Who looks inside, awakens.</u>

    <u>Carl Jung</u>

TAKE OVER — What needs to be awakened in you? What knowledge are you lacking to move forward? How are you going to attain it?

KEY WORDS
- knowledge
- eye of desire
- vision
- who looks outside, dreams
- who looks inside, awakens
- discovery
- pilot of the soul

ACROSTIC — PILOT OF THE SOUL

NOTES:
_____
_____
_____
_____
_____
_____
_____

Monday & Tuesday

WEEK 11: I WILL ACT NOW! CHANGE IS IMMINENT.
                                              -Og Mandinio

- <u>I will act now!</u> I will act now! I will act now! Henceforth I will repeat these words each hour, each day, <u>every day</u>, until the words become as much a habit as my breathing and the action which follows becomes as <u>instinctive</u> as the blinking of my eyelids. With these words I can <u>condition my mind</u> to perform every <u>action</u> necessary for my <u>success</u>. I will act now! I will repeat these words again and again. I will walk where failures fear to walk. I will work when the failure seeks rest. I will talk while the failure remains silent. <u>I will say done</u> before the failure says it's too late. I will act now. For now is all I have. Tomorrow is the day reserved for the labor of the lazy. I am not **lazy**. Tomorrow is the day when the failure will succeed. <u>I am not a **failure**</u>. Tomorrow is the day evil becomes good. I am not **evil**. I will act now. Success will not wait. Tomorrow is the day the weak become strong. I am not **weak**. If I delay, success will become wed to another and lost to me forever. This is the time. This is the place. <u>I am the person</u>.

TAKE OVER   -How will you "Act Now?" What will it look like?

KEY WORDS   -I will act now   -every day
                   -instinctive   -condition my mind
                   -action   -success
                   -I will say done   -I am not a failure
                   -I am the person   -imminent

ACROSTIC   -SUCCESS
                   -EVERY DAY

NOTES

NOTES

Wednesday & Thursday

WEEK 11: I WILL ACT NOW! CHANGE IS IMMINENT.

❖ **Don't be a LEWF**- Og Mandino

    I am not lazy, the LEWF said with a smile.
    It's all figured out, got it filed in my file.
    If I spend all today relaxing I'll bet,
    I'll be rested and ready for tomorrow to <u>sweat</u>.

    "Me, evil?" the LEWF said with a grin.
    How could you <u>utter</u> such nonsense, such a sin?
    Wait 'til the morrow, as idle minds would,
    Be out of my system, tomorrow's for good.

    So my <u>productivity</u> is down a little this month.
    And last month, last year...haven't you had a <u>slump</u>?
    "Weak?" the LEWF questioned, you insult me today!
    I can <u>choose to be strong</u> –is tomorrow okay?
    <u>Success is the banner</u> that hangs o'er my chair
    I see it, I read it, I shout in the air
    Can nobody hear me? I mean it this time!
    A failure? No! Tomorrow, success will be mine!

    And so we hear such repetitive <u>oration</u>,
    From LEWFs who love <u>procrastination</u>.
    But everyone knows the price they will pay.
    For when tomorrow is here, it will still be today.

TAKE OVER — Using the quote from Monday/Tuesday, what does "LEWF" stand for? Be sure to define/explain each underlined word.

KEY WORDS
- sweat
- productivity
- choose to be strong
- oration
- utter
- slump
- success is the banner
- procrastination

ACROSTIC:
- IMMINENT
- PRODUCTIVITY

Friday

WEEK 11: I WILL ACT NOW! CHANGE IS IMMINENT.

❖ **How do I change?**-Og Mandino

> If I feel depressed I will sing.
> If I feel sad I will laugh.
> If I feel ill I will double my labor.
> If I feel fear I will plunge ahead.
> If I feel inferior I will wear new garments.
> If I feel uncertain I will raise my voice.
> If I feel poverty I will think of wealth to come.
> If I feel incompetent I will think of past success.
> If I feel insignificant I will remember my goals.
> Today I will be the master of my emotions.

TAKE OVER -What do you need to change? Start now! Minute by minute, hour by hour, day by day...if you slip: start again.

KEY WORDS -I will

ACROSTIC -MASTER

NOTES:

___
___
___
___
___
___
___
___

Monday

WEEK 12: THERE'S NO SUBSTITUTE FOR HARD WORK (Thomas Edison)

❖ <u>Determination</u> and <u>perseverance</u> move the world; thinking that others will do it for you is a sure way to fail.

<u>Marva Collins</u>

TAKE OVER — What do you "allow" others to do FOR you that you can do yourself? Take control of your actions, you need it completed, you do it…you want to know it, you learn it…you want something, you persevere.

KEY WORDS — determination
— perseverance

ACROSTIC — PERSEVERANCE

NOTES:
_____
_____
_____
_____
_____
_____
_____

Tuesday

WEEK 12: THERE'S NO SUBSTITUTE FOR HARD WORK (Thomas Edison)

❖ Will you look back on life and say, 'I wish I had,' or 'I'm glad I did'?

Zig Ziglar

❖ Begin with the end in mind.

Stephen Covey

TAKE OVER -Explain the difference between "regretting" a past mistake and a past missed opportunity.

KEY WORDS -I wish I had
-I'm glad I did
-begin

ACROSTIC -BEGIN

NOTES:
_____
_____
_____
_____
_____
_____

Wednesday

WEEK 12: THERE'S NO SUBSTITUTE FOR HARD WORK (Thomas Edison)

> ❖ The miracle, or the power, that <u>elevates</u> the few is to be found in their perseverance under the promptings of a <u>brave</u>, <u>determined</u> spirit.
>
> <u>Mark Twain</u>

TAKE OVER — What is Mark Twain saying in this quote? Write 2-3 sentences in your own words. What point he is trying to get across. How is this "brave?"

KEY WORDS
- elevates
- perseverance
- brave
- determined

ACROSTIC — BRAVE

NOTES:
_____
_____
_____
_____
_____
_____
_____

Thursday

WEEK 12: THERE'S NO SUBSTITUTE FOR HARD WORK (Thomas Edison)

* The person who makes a success of living is the one who sees his goal <u>steadily</u> and aims for it <u>unswervingly</u>. That is <u>dedication</u>.

<u>Cecil B De Mille</u>

TAKE OVER -See the goal, write the goal, dream the goal, aim for the goal, and dedicate your actions to your goal. What is YOUR goal?

KEY WORDS -steadily
-unswervingly
-dedication

ACROSTIC -UNSWERVINGLY

NOTES:
_____
_____
_____
_____
_____
_____

Friday

WEEK 12: THERE'S NO SUBSTITUTE FOR HARD WORK (Thomas Edison)

- ❖ Every person who wins in any <u>undertaking</u> must be willing to <u>cut all sources of retreat</u>. Only by doing so can one be sure of maintaining that <u>state of mind</u> known as a <u>burning desire to win</u> – <u>essential</u> to success.

<u>Napoleon Hill</u>

TAKE OVER — What does "cut all sources of retreat" mean? What is your mind-set? Do you give up when it is hard? Do you look for ways out after you set a goal? OR, does hard motivate you, will you change your state of mind to succeed/WIN?

KEY WORDS
- undertaking
- cut all sources of retreat
- state of mind
- burning desire to win
- essential

ACROSTIC — UNDERTAKING

NOTES:
_____
_____
_____
_____
_____
_____
_____

Monday

WEEK 13: I will succeed! Step by Step

- ❖ <u>Making a success</u> of the job at hand is the <u>best step</u> toward the kind you want.

    <u>Bernard M. Baruch</u>

- ❖ The journey of a thousand miles must <u>begin</u> with a single step.

    <u>Chinese Proverb</u>

TAKE OVER -There is no better place to start than at the beginning.
-What is your first step going to be?

KEY WORDS -making a Success
-step
-begin

ACROSTIC -BEST STEP

NOTES:
_____
_____
_____
_____
_____
_____

Tuesday

WEEK 13: I will succeed! Step by Step

❖ There is no sudden leap into the <u>stratosphere</u>. There is only <u>advancing</u> step by step, slowly and <u>tortuously</u>, up the <u>pyramid</u> towards your goal.

<u>Ben Stein</u>

TAKE OVER -What is your goal again? What must the first step be?
-What is the second step?

KEY WORDS -stratosphere
-advancing
-tortuously
-pyramid

ACROSTIC -ADVANCING

NOTES:
_____
_____
_____
_____
_____
_____
_____

Wednesday

WEEK 13: I will succeed! Step by Step

- <u>Setting goals</u> is the <u>first step</u> in turning the invisible into the visible.

    <u>Anthony Robbins</u>

- Throughout the centuries there were men who took first steps, down <u>new roads</u>, <u>armed with nothing</u> but their own <u>vision</u>.

    <u>Ayn Rand</u>

TAKE OVER -What is YOUR vision? Map out the directions to attain your vision.

KEY WORDS
-setting Goals
-first Step
-new Roads
-armed with nothing
-vision

ACROSTIC -VISION

NOTES:
_____
_____
_____
_____
_____
_____
_____

Thursday

WEEK 13: I will succeed! Step by Step

❖ Life <u>affords</u> no higher pleasure than that of <u>surmounting</u> difficulties, passing from one step of success to another, <u>forming new wishes</u> and <u>seeing them gratified</u>.

<u>Samuel Johnson</u>

TAKE OVER -Part of setting goals and visions is you must include plans to overcome difficulties, obstacles, and barriers. What things or people do you see being a possible obstacle for you? How are you going to rise above and move forward?

KEY WORDS
-affords
-surmounting
-forming new wishes
-seeing them gratified

ACROSTIC -SURMOUNTING

NOTES:
_____
_____
_____
_____
_____
_____
_____

Friday

WEEK 13: I will succeed! Step by Step

- ❖ Develop an <u>attitude of gratitude</u>, and give thanks for everything that happens to you, knowing that every step forward is a step toward <u>achieving something bigger</u> and better than your current situation.

<u>Brian Tracy</u>

TAKE OVER -You must learn from everything; successes, failures, people, books, situations...
-What have you learned so far from each of the above?

KEY WORDS -attitude of Gratitude
-achieving Something Bigger

ACROSTIC -ATTITUDE OF GRATITUDE

NOTES:
_____
_____
_____
_____
_____
_____
_____

Monday

WEEK 14: We can't help everyone, but everyone can help someone.
Dr. Loretta Scott

❖ It's not what you've got; it's what you use that makes a difference.

Zig Ziglar

❖ It's easy to make a buck. It's a lot tougher to make a difference.

W. Clement Stone

TAKE OVER -What is the difference you will make today? What about tomorrow, the next day, the next day...plan to make a difference?

KEY WORDS -difference
-make a difference

ACROSTIC -MAKE A DIFFERENCE

NOTES:
_____
_____
_____
_____
_____
_____
_____

Tuesday

WEEK 14: We can't help everyone, but everyone can help someone.
<u>Dr. Loretta Scott</u>

❖ Remember, if you ever need a <u>helping hand</u>, you'll find one at the end of your arm...As you grow older you will <u>discover</u> that you have two hands. One for helping yourself, the other for helping others.

<u>Audrey Hepburn</u>

TAKE OVER -Whose life will you help today? What "favor" will you do for someone? Can you do it anonymously?

KEY WORDS -helping hand
-discover

ACROSTIC -HELPING OTHERS

NOTES:
_____
_____
_____
_____
_____
_____
_____

Wednesday

WEEK 14: We can't help everyone, but everyone can help someone.
Dr. Loretta Scott

- It is one of the most beautiful <u>compensations</u> of this life that no man can <u>sincerely</u> try to help another without helping himself.

    Ralph Waldo Emmerson

- You can have everything in life you want, if you will just <u>help</u> enough other people get what they want.

    Zig Ziglar

TAKE OVER — Explain what the two quotes are trying to say. Write down what meaning it has for you.

KEY WORDS
- compensation
- sincerely
- help

ACROSTIC — COMPENSATION

NOTES:

_____
_____
_____
_____
_____
_____
_____

Thursday

WEEK 14: We can't help everyone, but everyone can help someone.
Dr. Loretta Scott

- ❖ <u>Believe</u>, when you are most unhappy, that there is something for you to do in the world. So long as you can <u>sweeten another's pain</u>, <u>life is not in vain</u>.

    Helen Keller

- ❖ People will forget what you <u>said</u>, people will forget what you <u>did</u>, but people will never forget how you made them <u>feel</u>.

    Maya Angelou

TAKE OVER -Re-write the second quote and substitute a synonym for the underlined words. Can you focus on the positive of someone else's life while yours is in turmoil? Can you help someone else during times you are struggling? Explain your answers and why it would be beneficial if you could.

KEY WORDS -believe
-sweeten another's pain
-life is not in vain
-said-Did-Feel

ACROSTIC -BELIEVE

NOTES:
_____
_____
_____
_____
_____
_____

Friday

WEEK 14: We can't help everyone, but everyone can help someone.
Dr. Loretta Scott

- Success has nothing to do with what you gain in life or accomplish for yourself. It's what you do for others.

Danny Thomas

- Look up and not down. Look forward and not back. Look out and not in, and lend a hand.

Edward Everett Hale

TAKE OVER — Review this week's quotes and title. In a paragraph, write what this week's quotes have given you to think about. In paragraph two, write what you are going to do to become successful through helping others…how are you going to help others…details…make a plan…be intentional.

KEY WORDS
- success
- accomplish
- look up-Look forward-Look out
- lend a hand
- gain in life
- do for others

ACROSTIC — LEND A HAND

NOTES:
_____
_____
_____
_____
_____
_____

Monday

WEEK 15: A Hero is a man who is afraid to run away.
English Proverb

❖ How important it is for us to <u>recognize</u> and <u>celebrate</u> our <u>heroes</u> and <u>she-roes</u>!

Maya Angelou

❖ Heroes are people who rise to the <u>occasion</u> and <u>slip away quietly</u>.

Tom Brokov

TAKE OVER — Who is a true hero to you? Why, what makes that person a hero?

KEY WORDS
- recognize
- heroes
- occasion
- celebrate
- she-roes
- slip away quietly

ACROSTIC — HEROES

NOTES:
_____
_____
_____
_____
_____
_____

Tuesday

WEEK 15: A Hero is a man who is afraid to run away.
<u>English Proverb</u>

❖ You don't have to be a <u>fantastic</u> hero to do certain things – <u>to compete</u>. You can be just an <u>ordinary</u> <u>chap</u>, <u>sufficiently</u> <u>motivated</u> to reach <u>challenging</u> <u>goals</u>.

<u>Sir Edmund Hillary</u>

TAKE OVER -Do you believe in the "ordinary" doing the "extraordinary?" What would be an example? Please describe. What is the difference between goals and challenging goals? Explain.

KEY WORDS
-fantastic
-to compete
-ordinary chap
-sufficiently motivated
-challenging goals

ACROSTIC -COMPETE

NOTES:
___
___
___
___
___
___
___

Wednesday

WEEK 15: A Hero is a man who is afraid to run away.
<u>English Proverb</u>

❖ A hero is an ordinary individual who finds the strength to <u>persevere</u> and <u>endure</u> <u>in spite of</u> overwhelming <u>obstacles.</u>

<u>Christopher Reeve</u>

❖ Failures to heroic minds are the <u>stepping stones</u> to success.

<u>Thomas C. Halibuton</u>

TAKE OVER   -Explain Mr. Haliburton's quote.

KEY WORDS   -persevere
-endure
-in spite of
-obstacles
-stepping Stones

ACROSTIC   -STEPPING STONES

NOTES:
_____
_____
_____
_____
_____
_____

Thursday

WEEK 15: A Hero is a man who is afraid to run away.
<u>English Proverb</u>

❖ When the <u>will</u> <u>defies fear</u>, when <u>duty</u> throws the <u>gauntlet</u> down to <u>fate</u>, when <u>honor</u> <u>scorns</u> to <u>compromise</u> with death – that is heroism.

<u>Robert Green Ingersoll</u>

TAKE OVER —Throwing the gauntlet down, what does this mean? Have YOU ever done this?

KEY WORDS
- will
- duty
- fate
- compromise
- defies fear
- gauntlet
- honor scorns

ACROSTIC —GAUNTLET

NOTES:
_____
_____
_____
_____
_____
_____
_____

Friday

WEEK 15: A Hero is a man who is afraid to run away.
<u>English Proverb</u>

❖ The hero is one who <u>kindles</u> a <u>great light</u> in the world, who sets up <u>blazing torches</u> in the dark streets of life for men to see by.

<u>Felix Adler</u>

TAKE OVER   -Are you somebody's light? If you are, what actions would show that, what would it look like to someone "looking in from the outside?"

KEY WORDS   -kindles
-great Light
-blazing Torches

ACROSTIC   -GREAT LIGHT

NOTES:
_____
_____
_____
_____
_____
_____

Monday

WEEK 16: Out of difficulties grow Miracles.
<u>Jean De La Bruyre</u>

- Sometimes <u>adversity</u> is what you need to face in order to become <u>successful</u>.
  <u>Zig Ziglar</u>

- There are some <u>defeats</u> more triumphant than <u>victories</u>.
  <u>Michel Eyquem de Montaigne</u>

- Most of the <u>shadows</u> of this life are caused by standing in one's own sunshine.
  <u>Ralph Waldo Emerson</u>

- <u>Comfort</u> and <u>prosperity</u> have never <u>enriched</u> the world as much as <u>adversity</u> has.
  <u>Billy Graham</u>

TAKE OVER   -How is adversity able to make you better, more successful?

KEY WORDS
- adversity
- defeats
- shadows
- prosperity
- successful
- victories
- comfort
- enriched

ACROSTIC   -ADVERSITY

NOTES:
_____
_____
_____
_____
_____

Tuesday

WEEK 16: Out of difficulties grow Miracles.
Jean De La Bruyre

- Some minds seem almost to <u>create themselves</u>, <u>springing</u> up under every <u>disadvantage</u> and working their <u>solitary</u> but <u>irresistible</u> way through a thousand <u>obstacles.</u>

Washington Irving

- <u>Obstacles</u> can't stop you. Problems can't stop you. Most of all other people can't stop you. Only you can stop you.

Jeffrey Gitomer

TAKE OVER — How do you overcome an obstacle? Describe and make a plan for each obstacle, whether it is a person, a situation, time, limitations… Planning ahead will help when the obstacle appears. What possible adjustments to your plan will you need?

KEY WORDS
- create themselves
- springing
- disadvantage
- solitary
- irresistible
- obstacles

ACROSTIC — OBSTACLES

NOTES:
_____
_____
_____
_____
_____

Wednesday

WEEK 16: Out of difficulties grow Miracles.
<u>Jean De La Bruyre</u>

- You may not realize it when it happens, but a kick in the teeth may be the best thing in the world for you.

    <u>Walt Disney</u>

- <u>Adversity</u> has the effect of <u>eliciting talents</u>, which in <u>prosperous</u> circumstances would have <u>lain dormant</u>.

    <u>Horace</u>

TAKE OVER — How can losing be "the best thing in the world for you?" Describe a time when this took place in your life.

KEY WORDS
-adversity
-eliciting talents
-prosperous
-lain dormant

ACROSTIC -ELICITING TALENTS

NOTES:
_____
_____
_____
_____
_____
_____
_____

Thursday

WEEK 16: Out of difficulties grow Miracles.
<u>Jean De La Bruyre</u>

- ❖ <u>Achievement</u> is not always success, while <u>reputed failure</u> often is. It is <u>honest endeavor</u>, <u>persistent effort</u> to do the best possible under any and all <u>circumstances</u>.

    <u>Orison Swett Marden</u>

- ❖ Things don't go wrong and break your heart so you can become <u>bitter</u> and give up. They happen to break you down and build you up so you can be all that you were intended to be.

    <u>Charles "Tremendous" Jones</u>

TAKE OVER — Explain what you know about body building. Why must you "tear" your muscle to build it? How does body building relate to character building?

KEY WORDS
- achievement
- persistent effort
- honest endeavor
- reputed failure
- circumstances
- bitter

ACROSTIC — HONEST ENDEAVOR

NOTES:
_____
_____
_____
_____
_____
_____

Friday

WEEK 16: Out of difficulties grow Miracles.
<u>Jean De La Bruyre</u>

❖ Don't be afraid to fail. Don't waste energy trying to cover up <u>failure</u>. Learn from your failures and go on to the <u>next challenge</u>. It's OK to fail. <u>If you're not failing, you're not growing.</u>

<u>H. Stanley Judd</u>

❖ If we study the lives of great men and women carefully and unemotionally we find that, <u>invariably</u>, <u>greatness</u> was <u>developed</u>, tested and <u>revealed</u> through the darker periods of their lives. One of the largest <u>tributaries</u> of the <u>RIVER OF GREATNESS</u> is always the <u>STREAM OF ADVERSITY</u>.

<u>Cavett Robert</u>

TAKE OVER -Think about both quotes. Re-write the quotes into one quote using your own words.

KEY WORDS
- failure
- next Challenge
- If you're not failing, you're not growing.
- invariably
- developed
- revealed
- tributaries
- river of greatness
- stream of adversity

ACROSTIC -TRIBUTARIES

NOTES:
_____
_____
_____
_____
_____

Monday

WEEK 17: Every day, in every way, I am getting better and better.
Emily Coue

- You can't have a better tomorrow if you are thinking about yesterday all the time.
  Charles F. Kettering

- If you aren't <u>fired up</u> with <u>enthusiasm</u>, you'll be fired with enthusiasm.
  Vincent Lombardi

TAKE OVER -Explain what Kettering's quote is saying.

KEY WORDS -tomorrow
-yesterday
-fired up
-enthusiasm

ACROSTIC -ENTHUSIASM

NOTES:
_____
_____
_____
_____
_____
_____

Tuesday

WEEK 17: Every day, in every way, I am getting better and better.
Emily Coue

- ❖ Be willing to make <u>decisions</u>. That's the most important <u>quality</u> in a good <u>leader</u>. Don't fall victim to what I call the <u>Ready-Aim-Aim-Aim Syndrome</u>. You must be willing to fire.

    T. Boone Pickens

- ❖ Success is not the result of <u>spontaneous combustion</u>, you must set yourself on fire first.
    Reggie Leach

TAKE OVER — Do you hesitate when making decisions? Do you plan and have second thoughts? Set a goal, make a plan and move forward...don't look back.

KEY WORDS
- decisions
- quality
- leader
- ready-Aim-Aim-Aim Syndrome
- spontaneous combustion
- set yourself on fire (What does this mean?)

ACROSTIC — DECISIONS

NOTES:
_____
_____
_____
_____
_____
_____

Wednesday

WEEK 17: Every day, in every way, I am getting better and better.
Emily Coue

❖ The greatest amount of <u>wasted time</u> is the not getting started.

Dawson Trotman

❖ The mind is not a <u>vessel</u> to be filled, but a fire to be <u>kindled</u>.

Plutarch

❖ Each one of us has a <u>fire in our heart</u> for something. It's our goal in life to <u>find it</u> and to <u>keep it lit</u>.

Mary Lou Retton

TAKE OVER -What is your fire? Have you found it yet? What are you going to do about it?

KEY WORDS
-wasted time   -vessel
-kindled   -fire in our heart
-find it   -keep it lit

ACROSTIC -FIRE IN OUR HEART

NOTES:
_____
_____
_____
_____
_____
_____
_____

Thursday

WEEK 17: Every day, in every way, I am getting better and better.
Emily Coue

- ❖ The starting point of all <u>achievement</u> is <u>desire</u>. Keep this constantly in mind. Weak desires bring weak results, just as a small amount of fire makes a small amount of heat.

  Napoleon Hill

- ❖ The person who <u>sends out</u> positive thoughts <u>activates</u> the world around him positively and draws back to himself <u>positive results</u>.

  Norman Vincent Peale

TAKE OVER -Have you found your fire yet? What is it? Go get it.

KEY WORDS
-achievement   -desire
-sends out   -activates
-positive results

ACROSTIC -DESIRE

NOTES:
_____
_____
_____
_____
_____
_____
_____

Friday

WEEK 17: Every day, in every way, I am getting better and better.
Emily Coue

- In everyone's life, at some time, our <u>inner fire</u> goes out. It is then burst into flame by an <u>encounter</u> with another human being. We should all be thankful for those people who <u>rekindle</u> the inner spirit.

    Albert Schweitzer

- Work joyfully and peacefully, knowing that right thoughts and right efforts will <u>inevitably</u> bring about right results.

    James Allen

TAKE OVER -Once you know what your fire is; surround yourself with people (kindling) who can keep you lit. Those who act as a "wet rag" to dowse your fire; let them move aside. Who is your kindling?

KEY WORDS -inner fire
-encounter
-rekindle
-inevitably

ACROSTIC REKINDLE

NOTES:
_____
_____
_____
_____
_____
_____

IV. Self-Series-Weeks 18-20

Self-discipline is a form of freedom. Freedom from laziness and lethargy, freedom from expectations and demands of others, freedom from weakness and fear -- and doubt.

H. A. Dorfman

Weeks 18-20 is a "Self" Series

Monday

WEEK 18: SELF-CONTROL

❖ No man is free who is not <u>master</u> of himself.

<u>Epictetus</u>

❖ There is little that can <u>withstand</u> a man who can <u>conquer</u> himself.

<u>Louis XIV</u>

TAKE OVER — Explain what the quotes are trying to say. Why is it important to have control over yourself?

KEY WORDS
- master
- withstand
- conquer

ACROSTIC — CONQUER

NOTES:
_____
_____
_____
_____
_____
_____

Tuesday

WEEK 18: SELF-CONTROL

❖ No man is fit to <u>command</u> another who cannot command himself.

<u>William Penn</u>

❖ <u>Prudent</u>, <u>cautious</u> self-control is <u>wisdom's root</u>.

<u>Robert Burns</u>

TAKE OVER	-Prudent, cautious, what do these words say to you about self-control? What is another phrase/quote you can think of that re-states Penn's quotes?
KEY WORDS	-command -prudent -cautious -wisdom's root
ACROSTIC	-PRUDENT

NOTES:
___
___
___
___
___
___
___

Wednesday

WEEK 18: SELF-CONTROL

❖ The difference between <u>want</u> and <u>need</u> is self-control.

<u>Unknown</u>

❖ If A=success, then A=X+Y+Z, with X being work, Y being play and Z keeping your mouth shut.

<u>Albert Einstein</u>

TAKE OVER   -What do both of these quotes have in common? Explain your answer.

KEY WORDS   -want ⎤ What is the difference between these two words?
                           -need ⎦

ACROSTIC   -SELF CONTROL

NOTES:
_____
_____
_____
_____
_____
_____

Thursday

WEEK 18: SELF-CONTROL

- ❖ The best time to <u>hold your tongue</u> is the time you feel you must say something or bust.

<u>Josh Billings</u>

- ❖ The greatest <u>remedy</u> for anger is <u>delay</u>.

<u>Seneca</u>

TAKE OVER	-Think about the times you have been in a conflict/disagreement and responded quickly with words you later regretted. Also, think about times you didn't have a chance to respond and after time passed, the situation cooled and dispersed without regret. Which outcome was preferable? Express in writing.
KEY WORDS	-hold your tongue -remedy -delay
ACROSTIC	-DELAY

NOTES:

_____
_____
_____
_____
_____
_____
_____

Friday

WEEK 18: SELF-CONTROL

❖ The <u>cyclone</u> <u>derives</u> its power from a <u>calm center</u>. So does a person.

<u>Norman Vincent Peale</u>

❖ <u>Acts</u> that proceed from your <u>calm center</u> are always more effective than acts that <u>proceed</u> from fear, guilt or anger.

<u>Alan Cohen</u>

❖ The ability to <u>concentrate</u> and <u>use time</u> well is everything.

<u>Lee Iacocca</u>

TAKE OVER	-How would a "calm center" assist you in achieving your goals?
KEY WORDS	-cyclone derives -calm center -extra mile -concentrate -use time -acts -proceed
ACROSTIC	-EXTRA MILE

NOTES:
_____
_____
_____
_____
_____
_____

Monday

WEEK 19: DISCOVER SELF-IMPROVEMENT, GROW

❖ You have to leave the <u>city of your comfort</u> and go into the <u>wilderness of your intuition</u>. What you'll <u>discover</u> will be wonderful. What you'll discover is <u>yourself</u>.

<u>Alan Alda</u>

❖ What you <u>get</u> by <u>achieving</u> your goals is not as important as what you <u>become</u> by achieving your goals.

<u>Zig Ziglar</u>

TAKE OVER -Stepping out of your comfort zone to work towards your goal...how does this help?
-Each step towards your goal that you reach and surpass, how does that help you discover more about you?

KEY WORDS
- city of your comfort
- wilderness of your intuition
- yourself
- achieving
- discover
- get
- become

ACROSTIC -DISCOVER

NOTES:
_____
_____
_____
_____
_____
_____
_____

Tuesday

WEEK 19: DISCOVER SELF-IMPROVEMENT, GROW

❖ Do not bother to be better than your <u>contemporaries</u> or <u>predecessors</u>. Try to be better than yourself.

<u>William Faulkner</u>

❖ <u>Self-improvement</u> is the name of the game, and your <u>primary objective</u> is to <u>strengthen yourself</u>, not to destroy an opponent.

<u>Maxwell Maltz</u>

TAKE OVER   -What if you are up for a promotion and it is between you and one other person. What should your next move be and why?

KEY WORDS   -contemporaries   -predecessors   -tomorrow
-yesterday   -self-improvement
-primary objective   -strengthen yourself

ACROSTIC   -SELF IMPROVEMENT

NOTES:

_____
_____
_____
_____
_____
_____
_____
_____

Wednesday

WEEK 19: DISCOVER SELF-IMPROVEMENT, GROW

- Men are <u>anxious</u> to <u>improve</u> their <u>circumstances</u>, but are unwilling to improve themselves; they therefore remain <u>bound</u>.

  <u>James Allen</u>

- The biggest room in the world is the room for <u>improvement.</u>

  <u>Unknown</u>

- I am not what has happened to me. I am what I <u>choose</u> to <u>become</u>.

  <u>Carl Jung</u>

TAKE OVER — Combine the 3 quotes above, in your own words, to develop a quote for your improvement.

KEY WORDS
- anxious
- circumstances
- improvement
- choose
- improve
- bound
- unwilling
- become

ACROSTIC — CHOOSE

NOTES
_____
_____
_____
_____
_____
_____
_____

Thursday

WEEK 19: DISCOVER SELF-IMPROVEMENT, GROW

- ❖ To unlock the door to the <u>future</u>, you must first <u>possess</u> the <u>key</u> to the <u>past</u>.
  Unknown

- ❖ <u>Perfection</u> does not exist – you can always do better and you can always <u>grow</u>.
  Les Brown

- ❖ Don't just <u>seek</u> to discover who you are, <u>seek</u> to <u>determine</u> who you want to be.
  Bankole Williams

TAKE OVER
- Why is looking at your past important to guide your future?
- How will your past help you improve now?

KEY WORDS
- future   - possess   - key
- past   - perfection   - grow
- seek   - determine

ACROSTIC   -FUTURE

NOTES:
_____
_____
_____
_____
_____
_____

Friday

WEEK 19: DISCOVER SELF-IMPROVEMENT, GROW

- ❖ Some people say they haven't yet found themselves. But the <u>self</u> is not something one finds; it is something one <u>creates</u>.

    <u>Thomas Szasz</u>

- ❖ Unless you try to do something <u>beyond</u> what you have mastered, you will never <u>grow</u>.

    <u>C. R. Lawton</u>

TAKE OVER — What have you taken from this weeks' quotes? Describe a time when you went beyond your comfort zone and found a new hobby, friend, job?

KEY WORDS
- -self
- -beyond
- -creates
- -grow

ACROSTIC -BEYOND

NOTES:
_____
_____
_____
_____
_____
_____
_____

Monday

WEEK 20: BUILDING SELF-CONFIDENCE

- Too many people <u>overvalue</u> what they are not and <u>undervalue</u> what they are.

   <u>Malcom S. Forbes</u>

- <u>Respect</u> yourself if you would have others respect you.

   <u>Baltasar Gracian</u>

- The reason we <u>struggle</u> with <u>insecurity</u> is because we <u>compare</u> our behind-the-scenes with everyone else's <u>highlight reel</u>.

   <u>Steve Furtick</u>

TAKE OVER — Describe what these 3 quotes are saying to you. What are some scenes from YOUR highlight reel?

KEY WORDS
- overvalue
- respect
- insecurity
- highlight reel
- undervalue
- struggle
- compare

ACROSTIC — HIGHLIGHT REEL

NOTES:
_____
_____
_____
_____
_____
_____

Tuesday

WEEK 20: BUILDING SELF-CONFIDENCE

❖ <u>Outstanding</u> leaders go out of their way to <u>boost</u> the <u>self-esteem</u> of their <u>personnel</u>. If people believe in themselves, it's <u>amazing</u> what they can <u>accomplish</u>.

<u>Sam Walton</u>

❖ Whatever good things we <u>build</u> end up <u>building us</u>.

<u>Jim Rohn</u>

TAKE OVER   -Do you build up your friends, co-workers, family members, or perfect strangers? Give an example of how you can build each one of those people and how it would affect the relationship.

KEY WORDS
- outstanding
- self-esteem
- amazing
- building us
- boost
- personnel
- accomplish
- build

ACROSTIC   -BUILD

NOTES:

_____
_____
_____
_____
_____
_____

Wednesday

WEEK 20: BUILDING SELF-CONFIDENCE

❖ <u>Self-respect</u> <u>permeates</u> every <u>aspect</u> of your life.

<u>Joe Clark</u>

❖ Give me where to stand, and I will <u>move the earth</u>.

<u>Archimedes</u>

❖ <u>Confidence</u> is <u>contagious</u>, so is lack of confidence.

<u>Vince Lombardi</u>

TAKE OVER   -What are people going to "catch" from you?

KEY WORDS
- -self-respect
- -aspect
- -confidence
- -permeates
- -move the earth
- -contagious

ACROSTIC   -CONTAGIOUS

NOTES:
_____
_____
_____
_____
_____
_____

Thursday

WEEK 20: BUILDING SELF-CONFIDENCE

- ❖ Self-confidence is the most attractive <u>quality</u> a person can have. How can anyone see how great you are if you can't <u>see it</u> <u>yourself</u>?

    <u>Unknown</u>

- ❖ <u>Confidence</u>, like art, never comes from having all the answers; it comes from being open to all the questions.

    <u>Earl Gray Stevens</u>

- ❖ You can <u>determine</u> how <u>confident</u> people are by listening to what they DON'T say about themselves.

    <u>Brian G. Jett</u>

TAKE OVER — Growing in knowledge, talent and heart all help build confidence. What is holding you back? What is your fear? Describe it and overcome it.

KEY WORDS
- confidence
- see it
- doubt
- yourself
- quality
- determine

ACROSTIC — YOURSELF

NOTES:
_____
_____
_____
_____
_____
_____

111

Friday

WEEK 20: BUILDING SELF-CONFIDENCE

- Somehow I can't believe that there are any <u>heights</u> that can't be scaled by a man who knows the secrets of making dreams come true. This special secret, it seems to me, can be summarized in four Cs. They are <u>curiosity</u>, <u>confidence</u>, <u>courage</u>, and <u>consistency</u> and the greatest of all is confidence. When you <u>believe</u> in a thing, believe in it all the way, <u>implicitly</u> and <u>unquestionably</u>.

<u>Walt Disney</u>

- You have to have <u>confidence</u> in your <u>ability</u>, and then be <u>tough</u> enough to <u>follow through</u>.

<u>Rosalyn Carter</u>

- You <u>gain</u> <u>strength</u>, <u>courage</u> and <u>confidence</u> by every <u>experience</u> in which you really stop to look fear in the face. Do the thing you think you cannot do.

<u>Eleanor Roosevelt</u>

- <u>Confidence</u>…thrives on <u>honesty</u>, on <u>honor</u>, on the <u>sacredness</u> of <u>obligations</u>, on <u>faithful protection</u> and on <u>unselfish performance</u>. Without them, it cannot live.

<u>Franklin Roosevelt</u>

TAKE OVER   -What is your plan now? How is your journey going to begin?

KEY WORDS   -all underlined words

ACROSTIC   -SELF-CONFIDENCE

NOTES:

_____
_____
_____
_____

V. African American Leaders-Motivational Quotes

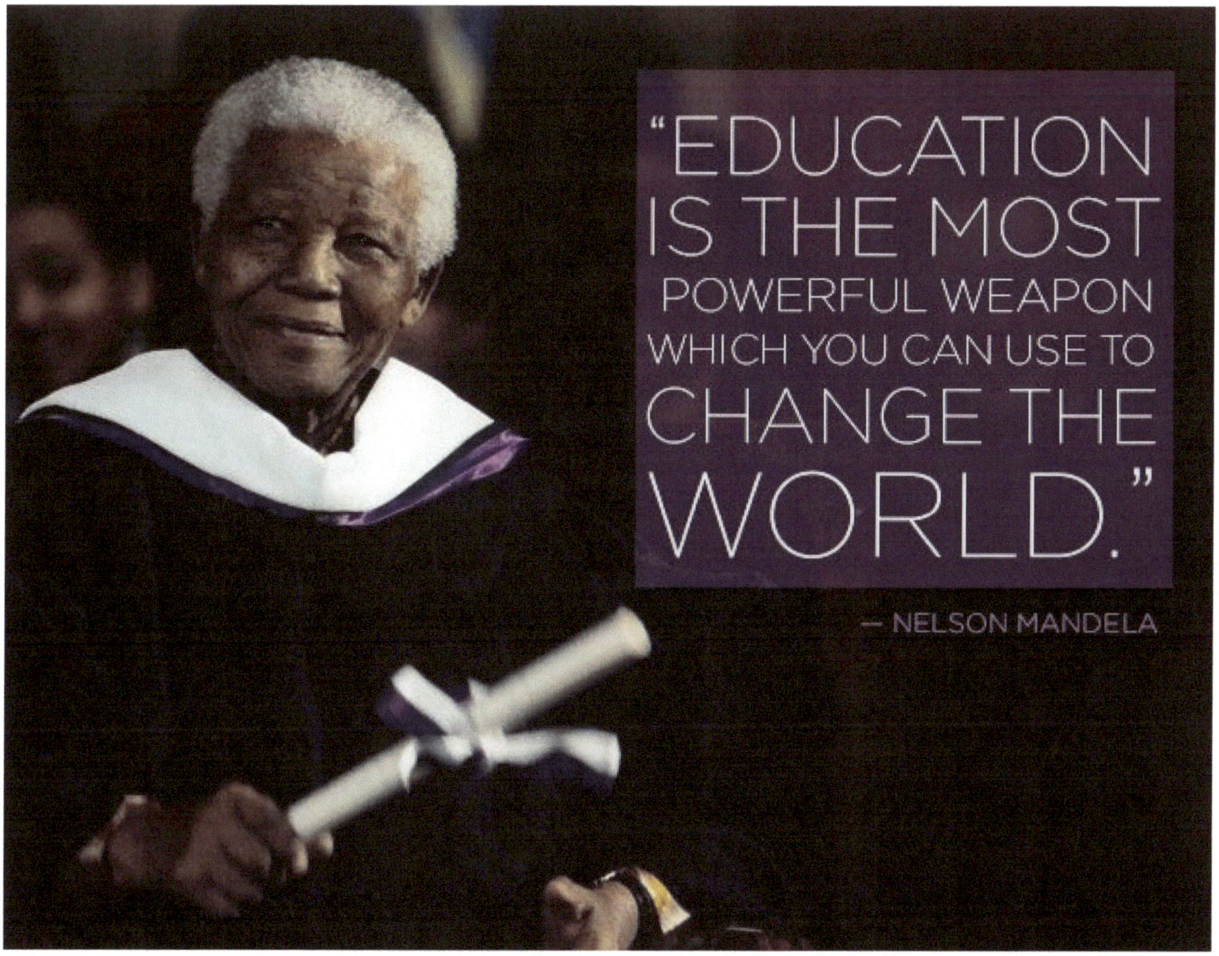

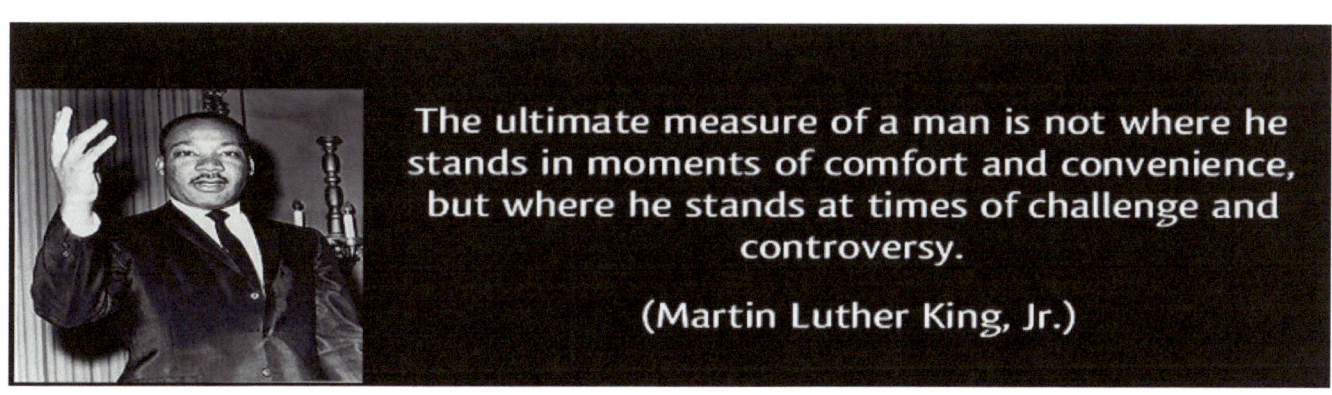

African American Leaders' Motivational Quotes

Leaders included:

Booker T. Washington	Maya Angelou	Harriet Tubman
Martin Luther King Jr.	Coretta Scott King	Phylicia Rashad
Fredrick Douglas	George Washington Carver	Jesse Owens
Jackie Joyner Kersee	Langston Hughes	Muhammad Ali
W. E. B. DuBois	Jackie Robinson	Shirley Chisholm
Michael Jordan	James A. Baldwin	Whoopi Goldberg
Oprah Winfrey	Colin Powell	Barbara Jordan
Satchel Paige	Pele	Larry Fitzgerald

Maya Angelou

=One isn't necessarily born with <u>courage</u>, but one is born with <u>potential</u>. Courage is the most important of all the <u>virtues</u>, because without courage you can't <u>practice</u> any other virtue <u>consistently</u>. You can practice virtue <u>erratically</u>, but nothing consistently without courage.

=I've learned that people will forget what you said, people will forget what you did, but people will never forget how you made them feel.

=If you don't like something, change it. If you can't change it, change your <u>attitude</u>.

=My <u>great hope</u> is to laugh as much as I cry; to get my work done and try to love somebody and have the courage to accept the love in return.

=<u>Prejudice</u> is a <u>burden</u> that <u>confuses</u> the past, <u>threatens</u> the future and <u>renders</u> the present <u>inaccessible</u>.

Harriet Tubman

=Every <u>great dream</u> begins with a dreamer. Always remember, you have <u>within</u> you the <u>strength</u>, the <u>patience</u>, and the <u>passion</u> to reach for the stars to change the world

=I freed a thousand slaves. I could have freed a thousand more <u>if only they knew they were slaves</u>.

Jackie Robinson

=Life is not a spectator sport. If you're going to spend your whole life in the grandstand just watching what goes on, in my opinion you're wasting your life.

Fredrick Douglass

=I prefer to be true to myself, even at the hazard of incurring the ridicule of others, rather than to be false, and to incur my own abhorrence.

=If there is no struggle, there is no progress.

Coretta Scott King

=Freedom and justice cannot be parceled out in pieces to suit political convenience. I don't believe you can stand for freedom for one group of people and deny it to others.

=Hate is too great a burden to bear. It injures the hater more than it injures the hated.

=Segregation was wrong when it was forced by white people, and I believe it is still wrong when it is requested by black people.

George Washington Carver

=Fear of something is at the root of hate for others, and hate within will eventually destroy the hater.

=How far you go in life depends on your being tender with the young, compassionate with the aged, sympathetic with the striving and tolerant of the weak and strong. Because someday in your life you will have been all of these.

=Ninety-nine percent of the failures come from people who have the habit of making excuses.

=There is no short cut to achievement. Life requires thorough preparation – veneer isn't worth anything.

=When you can do the common things of life in an uncommon way, you will command the attention of the world.

=Where there is no vision, there is no hope.

Langston Hughes

=Hold fast to your dreams, for without them life is a broken winged bird that cannot fly.

=I will not take "but" for an answer.

Whoopi Goldberg

=An actress can only play a woman. I'm an actor, <u>I can</u> play anything.

=I am the <u>American Dream</u>. I am the <u>epitome</u> of what the American Dream basically said. It said, you could come from anywhere and be anything you want in this country. That's exactly what I've done.

=I am where I am because I <u>believe</u> in all <u>possibilities</u>.

Muhammad Ali

=A rooster crows only when it sees the light. Put him in the dark and he'll never crow. I have seen the light and I'm crowing.

=Hating people because of their color is wrong. And it doesn't matter which color does the hating. It's just plain wrong.

=I hated every minute of training, but I said, "Don't quit. Suffer now and live the rest of your life as a <u>champion</u>."

=Champions aren't made in the gyms. Champions are made from something they have deep inside them: A <u>desire</u>, a <u>dream</u>, a <u>vision</u>. They have to have <u>late minute stamina</u>, they have to be a little faster, they have to have the <u>skill</u> and the <u>will</u>. But the will must be stronger than the will.

=Only a man who knows what it is like to be <u>defeated</u> can reach down to the <u>bottom of his soul</u> and come up with the <u>extra ounce of power</u> it takes to win when the match is even.

Michael Jordan

=I can accept failure, everyone fails at something. But I can't accept <u>not trying</u>.

=I have always believed that if you put in the work, the results will come.

=I've missed more than 9000 shots in my career. I've lost almost 300 games. 26 times, I've been trusted to take the game winning shot and missed. I've failed over and over and over again in my life. And that is why I succeed.

=If you're trying to <u>achieve</u>, there will be <u>roadblocks</u>. I've had them; everybody has had them. But <u>obstacles</u> don't have to stop you. If you run into a wall, don't turn around and give up. <u>Figure out</u> how to <u>climb it</u>, <u>go through it</u>, or <u>work around it</u>.

=My <u>attitude</u> is that if you push me towards something that you think is a weakness, then I will turn that <u>perceived</u> weakness into a strength.

Jackie Joyner-Kersee

=It's better to look ahead and prepare than to look back and regret.

Rosa Parks

=At the time I was arrested I had no idea it would turn into this. It was just like any other day. The only thing that made it <u>significant</u> was that the <u>masses of the people</u> <u>joined in</u>.

=I have learned over the years that when one's mind is made up, this <u>diminishes</u> fear; knowing what must be done does away with <u>fear</u>.

Barbara Jordan

=A nation is formed by the <u>willingness</u> of each of us to <u>share</u> in the <u>responsibility</u> for <u>upholding</u> the <u>common good</u>.

=Do not call for black power or green power. Call for <u>brain power</u>.

=Let each person do his or her part. If one <u>citizen</u> is unwilling to <u>participate</u>, all of us are going to <u>suffer</u>. For the <u>American idea</u>, though it is shared by all of us, is <u>realized</u> in each one of us.

Oprah Winfrey

=Breathe. Let go. And remind yourself that this very moment is the only one you know you have for sure.

=Do the one thing you think you cannot do. Fail at it. Try again. Do better the second time. The only people who never tumble are those who never mount the high wire. This is your moment. Own it.

=I am a woman in process. I'm just trying like everybody else. I try to take every conflict, every experience, and learn from it. Life is never dull.

=I don't think of myself as a poor deprived ghetto girl who made good. I think of myself as somebody who from an early age knew I was responsible for myself, and I had to make good.

=I don't think you ever stop giving. I really don't. I think it's an on-going process. And it's not just about being able to write a check. It's being able to touch somebody's life.

Colin Powell

=Giving back involves a certain amount of giving up.

Satchel Paige

=Ain't no man can avoid being born average, but ain't no man got to be common.

James A. Baldwin

=Fires can't be made with dead embers, nor can enthusiasm be stirred by spiritless men. Enthusiasm in our daily work lightens effort and turns even labor into pleasant tasks.

=Hatred, which could destroy so much, never failed to destroy the man who hated, and this was an immutable law.

=I've always believed that you can think positive just as well as you can think negative.

Larry Fitzgerald

=I do what I am coached to do. That's part of being a team leader and captain. The job will change week in and week out, and it's not for you to question what your job is – it's to go out there and execute your assignments.

=When success finds you, it's because you were looking for it.

=This is a commitment. Do not give up because it's hard. Do it because you want it.

=To be great, you have to out work the man next to you.

Shirley Chisholm

=You don't make progress by standing on the sidelines, whimpering and complaining. You make progress by implementing ideas.

W. E. B. DuBois

=A little less complaint and whining, and a little more dogged work and manly striving, would do us more credit than a thousand civil rights bills.

Jesse Owens

=A lifetime of training for just ten seconds.

=Find the good. It's all around you. Find it, showcase it and you'll start believing in it.

=Friendships born on the field of athletic strife are the real gold of competition. Awards become corroded, friends gather no dust.

=Life doesn't give you all the practice races you need.

=The battles that count aren't the ones for gold medals. The struggles within yourself-the invisible, inevitable battles inside all of us-that's where it's at.

=We all have dreams. But in order to make dreams come into reality, it takes an awful lot of determination, dedication, self-discipline, and effort.

Phylicia Rashad

=The stubbornness I had as a child has been transformed into perseverance. I can let go but I don't give up. I don't beat myself up about negative things.

=There's always something to suggest that you'll never be who you wanted to be. Your choice is to take it or keep moving.

Martin Luther King Jr.

=One day we must come to see that peace is not merely a distant goal we seek, but that it is a means by which we arrive at the goal. We must pursue peaceful ends through peaceful means.

=We have flown the air like birds and swum the sea like fishes, but have yet to learn the simple as of walking the earth like brothers.

=Life's most persistent and urgent question is: What are you doing for others?

=We must accept finite disappointment, but we must never lose infinite hope.

=The quality, not the longevity, of one's life is what is important.

=Darkness cannot drive out darkness; only light can do that. Hate cannot drive out hate; only love can do that.

=Aspire to inspire before you expire.

=Everyone has the power of greatness. Not for fame, but greatness, because greatness is determined by service.

=All labor that uplifts humanity has dignity and importance and should be undertaken with painstaking excellence.

=An individual has not started living until he can rise above the narrow confines of his individualistic concerns to the broader concerns of all humanity.

=Every man must decide whether he will walk in the light of creative altruism or in the darkness of destructive selfishness.

=Have we not come to such an impasse in the modern world that we must love our enemies – or else? The chain reaction of evil – hate begetting hate, wars producing wars – must be broken, or else we shall be plunged into the dark abyss of annihilation.

Martin Luther King Jr.

=Human progress is neither automatic nor inevitable…Every step toward the goal of justice requires sacrifice, suffering, and struggle; the tireless exertions and passionate concern of dedicated individuals.

=I believe that unarmed truth and unconditional love will have the final word in reality. This is why right, temporarily defeated, is stronger than evil triumphant.

=In the end, we will remember not the words of our enemies, but the silence of our friends.

=Nonviolence is a powerful and just weapon; which cuts without wounding and ennobles the man who wields it. It is a sword that heals.

=That old law about 'an eye for an eye' leaves everybody blind. The time is always right to do the right thing.

=It's better to look ahead and prepare than to look back and regret.

=The ultimate measure of a man is not where he stands in moments of comfort and convenience, but where he stands at times of challenge and controversy.

=The ultimate tragedy is not the oppression and cruelty by the bad people but the silence over that by the good people.

=Whatever affects one directly, affects all indirectly. I can never be what I ought to be until you are what you ought to be. This is interrelated structure of reality.

Booker T. Washington

=I will permit no man to narrow and degrade my soul by making me hate him.

=Nothing ever comes to one, that is worth having, except as a result of hard work.

=I have learned that success is to be measured not so much by the position that one has reached in life as by the obstacles which he has had to overcome while trying to succeed.

=Character, not circumstances, makes the man.

=If you want to lift yourself up, lift someone else up.

Booker T. Washington

=You can't hold a man down without staying down with him.
No greater injury can be done to any youth than to let him feel that because he belongs to this or that race he will be advanced in life regardless of his <u>own merits</u> or <u>efforts</u>.

=Character is power.

=Nothing ever comes to one, that is worth having, except as a result of <u>hard work</u>.

=Associate yourself with people of good <u>quality</u>, for it is better to be alone than in bad company.

=No race can prosper 'til it learns that there is as much dignity in tilling a field as in writing a poem.

=Few things help an individual more than to place responsibility upon him, and to let him know that you trust him.

=Any man's life will be filled with constant and unexpected <u>encouragement</u> if he makes up his mind to do his <u>level best</u> each day.

Pele

=<u>Success</u> is no accident. It is <u>hard work</u>, <u>perseverance</u>, <u>learning</u>, <u>studying</u>, <u>sacrifice</u>, and most of all, love of what you are doing or learning to do.

=<u>Enthusiasm</u> is everything. It must be <u>taut</u> and vibrating like a guitar string.

=The more difficult the <u>victory</u>, the greater the happiness in winning.

=There is always someone out there getting <u>better</u> than you by training harder than you.

=You must <u>respect</u> people and work hard to be in shape. And I used to train very hard.

=When the other players went to the beach after training, <u>I was here</u> kicking the ball.

VI. Hispanic Leaders-Motivational Quotes

"Preservation of one's own culture does not require contempt or disrespect for other cultures." - Cesar Chavez

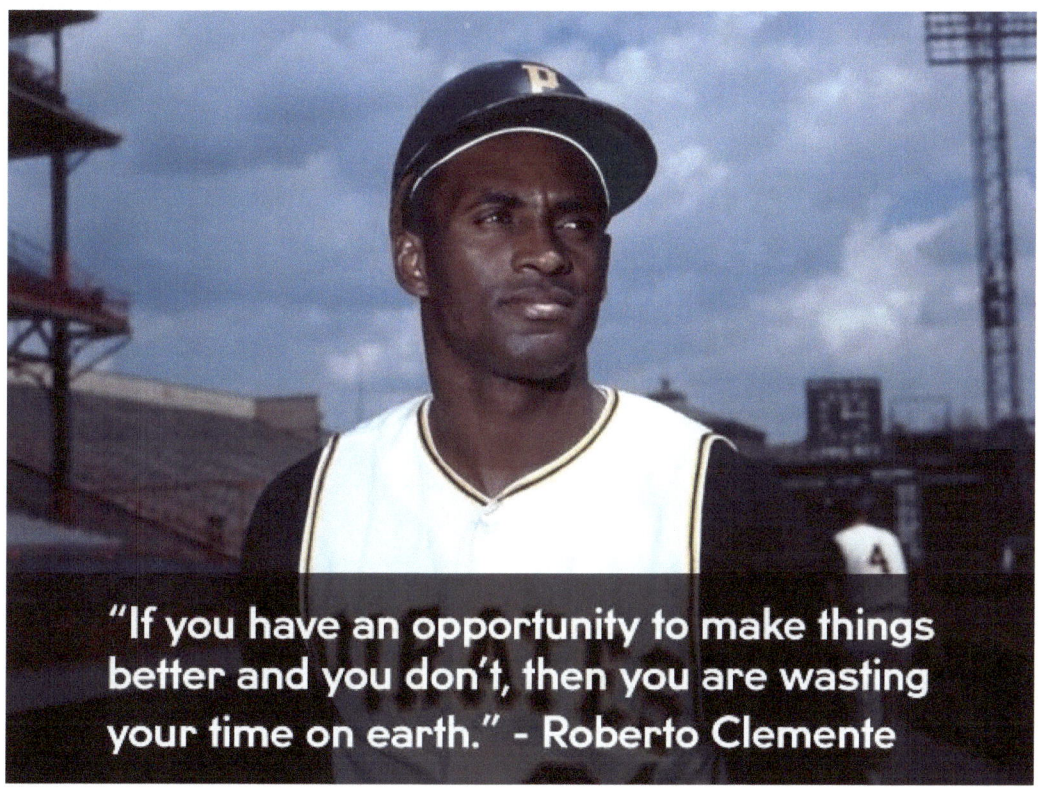

"If you have an opportunity to make things better and you don't, then you are wasting your time on earth." - Roberto Clemente

Motivational Hispanic Leaders' Quotes

Leaders included:

Jaime Escalante	Sonya Sotomayer	Cesar Chavez
Charlie Sheen	Jennifer Lopez	Alex Rodriguez
Mel Martinez	Geraldo Rivera	Desi Arnaz
Bill Richardson	Carlos Santana	Benito Juarez
Ricardo Montalban	Jimmy Smits	Martin Sheen
Edward James Olmos	Salma Hayek	Roberto Goizueta
Chi Chi Rodriguez	Henry Cisneros	Alberto Salazar
Ellen Ochoa		

Jaime Escalante (Stand and Deliver)

=The day someone quits school he is condemning himself to a future of poverty.

=That's the point. It goes like this: Teaching is touching life.

=One of the greatest things you have in life is that no one has the authority to tell you what you want to be. You're the one who'll decide what you want to be. Respect yourself and respect the integrity of others as well. The greatest thing you have is your self-image, a positive opinion of yourself. You must never let anyone take it from you.

=There will be no free rides, no excuses. You already have two strikes against you: your name and your complexion. Because of those two strikes, there are some people in this world who will assume that you know less than you do. *Math* is the great equalizer… When you go for a job, the person giving you that job will not want to hear your problems; ergo, neither do I. You're going to work harder here than you've ever worked anywhere else. And the only thing I ask from you is *ganas.* *Desire.* (from the movie)

Cesar Chavez

=From the <u>depth</u> of need and despair, people can work together, can organize themselves to <u>solve</u> their own problems and fill their own needs with <u>dignity</u> and <u>strength</u>.

=If you really want to <u>make a friend</u>, go to someone's house and eat with him... the people who give you their food give you their heart.

=In some cases non-violence requires more <u>militancy</u> than violence.

=Our language is the reflection of ourselves. A language is an exact reflection of the <u>character</u> and growth of its speakers.

=<u>Preservation</u> of one's own culture does not require contempt or disrespect for other cultures.

=Real education should consist of <u>drawing the goodness</u> and the best out of our own students. What better books can there be than the book of humanity?

=Students must have <u>initiative</u>; they should not be <u>mere</u> imitators. They must learn to <u>think</u> and <u>act</u> for themselves - and be free.

Jennifer Lopez

=Beauty is only skin deep. I think what's really important is finding a <u>balance</u> of mind, body and spirit.

=I'd be stupid not to take into consideration that there are certain things people will not consider me for because my name is Lopez. And I know I can do any kind of role. I don't want anybody to say, Oh, she can't pull this off. So those are <u>barriers</u> that you have to <u>overcome</u>.

=The bear is what we all wrestle with. Everybody has their <u>bear in life</u>. It's about <u>conquering</u> that bear and <u>letting him go</u>.

Mel Martinez

=Forty-two years ago, I came to America from communist Cuba so I might have a <u>better way of life</u>, a <u>freer way</u> of life - a more <u>democratic</u> way of life. I wanted to live the <u>American Dream</u> where if you <u>work hard</u> and put your mind to the task, anything was possible.

Desi Arnaz

=Good things do not come easy. The road is lined with pitfalls.

=Nobody bats 500. We all make mistakes.

=One of my biggest problems with comedy was that I did not understand some of the jokes.

=Since I was very young I have always worked hard at whatever I have had to do.

Carlos Santana

=Most people are <u>prisoners</u>, thinking only about the <u>future</u> or <u>living in the past</u>. They are not in the present, and the <u>present</u> is where everything <u>begins</u>.

=The most valuable possession you can own is an <u>open heart</u>. The most powerful weapon you can be is an <u>instrument of peace</u>.

Salma Hayek

=I proved to myself that if I <u>believe</u> in something and <u>set my mind</u> to it I could actually <u>accomplish</u> it.

=People often say that 'beauty is in the eye of the beholder, and I say that the most liberating thing about beauty is realizing that <u>you are the beholder</u>. This <u>empowers</u> us to find beauty in places where others have not dared to look, including <u>inside</u> ourselves.

=What is important is to believe in something so strongly that you're never discouraged.

Benito Juarez

=<u>Respect</u> for the <u>rights of others</u> means <u>peace</u>.

Ellen Ochoa

=I tell students that the opportunities I had were a result of having a good educational background. Education is what allows you to stand out.

=What everyone in the astronaut corps shares in common is not gender or ethnic background, but motivation, perseverance, and desire - the desire to participate in a voyage of discovery.

Henry Cisneros

=Americans are a can-do people, an enthusiastic people, a problem-solving people. And when given a direction and given a plan, they'll sign on.

Roberto Goizueta

=Once you lose everything, what's the worst that's going to happen to you? You develop a self-assurance.

=We're going to take risks. What has always been will not necessarily always be forever.

Ricardo Montalban

=If you shake your fist, the other guy will shake his too. But if you extend your hand to shake their hand, then they will extend theirs also, and you've made a friend.

Edward James Olmos

=A saint is a person who gives of themself without asking for anything in return. That's how simple it is to be a saint. Try it! Try being a saint.

=Education is the vaccine for violence.

=I believe that Gandhi was correct. Non-violent civil disobedience is the only way to bring about change that allows people to enjoy the change and not get killed in the process.

=I don't support violence, period.

=I learned to discipline myself to do things I didn't want to do.

Edward James Olmos

=Now I also discipline myself to do things I love to do when I don't want to do them.

=Our inability to relate to one another is very, very, very important. When we don't have it, we get into situations.

Bill Richardson

=Education enables people and societies to be what they can be.

=I choose bold. I choose action. I choose what's right for the people. I choose to make a difference.

=Ignorance has always been the weapon of tyrants; enlightenment the salvation of the free.

Geraldo Rivera

=Your performance gets you promoted. It doesn't matter if you're brown, black or white.

Alex Rodriguez

=Enjoy your sweat because hard work doesn't guarantee success, but without it you don't have a chance.

=Winners live in the present tense. People who come up short are consumed with future or past. I want to be living in the now.

Alex Rodriguez

=This is how I define grace: you're on the main stage, and it looks like it has been rehearsed 100 times, everything goes so smoothly. That's where I get my confidence and success, from knowing that I have an edge because I know I'm prepared.

Chi Chi Rodriguez

=Golf is a thinking man's game. You can have all the shots in the bag, but if you don't know what to do with them, you've got troubles.

=Only fools live in the past or carry envy to the present.

=The sweetest two words are 'next time.' The sourest word is 'if.'

Alberto Salazar

=An athlete who tells you the training is always easy and always fun, simply hasn't been there. Goals can be elusive which makes the difficult journey all the more rewarding.

=Early in my career I was accused of being overconfident and even cocky, but I really was confident that I had done the training and didn't see any other reason to say otherwise.

=I've run a lot of miles over the years, some fast and some not so fast. I've won some big races and I've had some big disappointments, but I enjoy the freedom of running and the challenge of training and competition as much now as when I first started back in high school.

=If you want to achieve a high goal, you're going to have to take some chances.

Charlie Sheen

=I just don't want to live like I used to. And at some point, I'm going to put a gag order on myself in terms of talking about the past. I've got to slam the door and deal with the present and the future.

=Uncertainty is a sign of humility, and humility is just the ability or the willingness to learn.

Martin Sheen

=I never went to college when I was young and am looking forward to giving it a try... at age 65!

=What we try to say is that it doesn't matter if you are a Republican or a Democrat or conservative or independent. You are <u>equally responsible</u> for your place in the culture, and you must make a contribution, and you must <u>accept responsibility</u> for what goes down on your watch.

Jimmy Smits

=I am a <u>firm believer</u> in <u>education</u> and have <u>worked</u> very hard to tell young Latinos that they must go to college and that, if possible, they should pursue an advanced degree. I am convinced that education is the <u>great equalizer</u>.

=It's less about the <u>physical training</u>, in the end, than it is about the <u>mental preparation</u>: boxing is a chess game. You have to be <u>skilled</u> enough and have <u>trained</u> hard enough to know how many different ways you can counterattack in any situation, at any moment.

=You have to find what makes you <u>stable</u> in the storm. Then, no matter what's happening round you, no matter what the hype or the publicity, you can still manage to <u>make leaps</u> in your work as an artist.

Sonia Sotomayor

=I want to state upfront, <u>unequivocally</u> and without doubt: I do not believe that any racial, ethnic or gender group has an advantage in sound judging. I do believe that every person has an <u>equal opportunity</u> to be a <u>good and wise</u> judge, regardless of their background or life experiences.

=I was raised in a Bronx public housing project, <u>but</u> studied at two of the nation's finest universities. I did work as an assistant district attorney, prosecuting violent crimes that devastate our communities.

VII. Coaches-Motivational Quotes

  **Pat Summitt's Definite Dozen**

1.	Respect Yourself and Others
2.	Take Full Responsibility
3.	Develop and Demonstrate Loyalty
4.	Learn to be a Great Communicator
5.	Discipline Yourself so No One Else Has To
6.	Make Hard Work Your Passion
7.	Don't Just Work Hard, Work Smart
8.	Put the Team Before Yourself
9.	Make Winning an Attitude
10.	Be a Competitor
11.	Change is a Must
12.	Handle Success Like You Handle Failure

Motivational Coaches' Quotes

Coaches included:

Pat Summit
John Wooden
Tony Dungy
Chuck Noll
Lou Holtz
Don Shula
Bobby Bowden
Jimmy Johnson

Bear Bryant
Joe Paterno
Vince Lombardi
Bobby Knight
Pat Riley
Tommy Lasorda
Woody Hayes
Tom Landry

Bear Bryant-College Football Coach

=Never quit. It is the easiest cop-out in the world. Set a goal and don't quit until you attain it. When you do attain it, set another goal, and don't quit until you reach it. Never quit.

John Wooden-College Basketball Coach

=A coach is someone who can give correction without causing resentment.

=Ability is a poor man's wealth.

=Adversity is the state in which man most easily becomes acquainted with himself, being especially free of admirers then.

=Be more concerned with your character than your reputation, because your character is what you really are, while your reputation is merely what others think you are.

=Be prepared and be honest.

=Consider the rights of others before your own feelings, and the feelings of others before your own rights.

=Do not let what you cannot do interfere with what you can do.

=Don't measure yourself by what you have accomplished, but by what you should have accomplished with your ability.

John Wooden-College Basketball Coach

=<u>Failure is not fatal</u>, but failure to change might be.

=I'd rather have a lot of <u>talent</u> and a little <u>experience</u> than a lot of experience and a little talent.

=If you don't have <u>time to do it right</u>, when will you have time to do it over?

=It isn't what you do, but <u>how you do it</u>.

=It's what you <u>learn after</u> you know it all that counts.

=If you're not making <u>mistakes</u>, then you're not doing anything. I'm positive that a <u>doer</u> makes mistakes.

=It's not so important who <u>starts</u> the game but who <u>finishes</u> it.

=It's the <u>little details that are vital</u>. Little things make big things happen.

=*Material possessions, winning scores, and great reputations are meaningless in the eyes of the Lord, because He knows what we really are and that is all that matters.*

=Never mistake <u>activity</u> for <u>achievement</u>.

=<u>Success</u> is never <u>final</u>, <u>failure</u> is never <u>fatal</u>. It's <u>courage</u> that counts.

=<u>Success</u> is <u>peace of mind</u> which is a <u>direct result</u> of self-satisfaction in knowing you did <u>your best</u> to become the best you are <u>capable</u> of <u>becoming</u>.

=*Talent is God given. Be humble. Fame is man-given. Be grateful. Conceit is self-given. Be careful.*

=The <u>main ingredient</u> of stardom is the rest of the team.

=*There are many things that are essential to arriving at true peace of mind, and one of the most important is faith, which cannot be acquired without prayer.*

=Things turn out best for the people who make the best of the way things turn out.

=What you are as a person is far more important that what you are as a basketball player.

John Wooden-College Basketball Coach

=Winning takes talent, to repeat takes character.

=You can't let praise or criticism get to you. It's a weakness to get caught up in either one.

=You can't live a perfect day without doing something for someone who will never be able to repay you.

Vince Lombardi-NFL

=Confidence is contagious. So is lack of confidence.

=Dictionary is the only place that success comes before work. Hard work is the price we must pay for success. I think you can accomplish anything if you're willing to pay the price.

=Fatigue makes cowards of us all.

=Football is like life - it requires perseverance, self-denial, hard work, sacrifice, dedication and respect for authority.

=I firmly believe that any man's finest hour, the greatest fulfillment of all that he holds dear, is that moment when he has worked his heart out in a good cause and lies exhausted on the field of battle - victorious.

=If winning isn't everything, why do they keep score?

=If you aren't fired with enthusiasm, you will be fired with enthusiasm.

=If you can accept losing, you can't win.

=Individual commitment to a group effort - that is what makes a team work, a company work, a society work, a civilization work.

=It's easy to have faith in yourself and have discipline when you're a winner, when you're number one. What you got to have is faith and discipline when you're not a winner.

=It's not whether you get knocked down, it's whether you get up.

=Once you learn to quit, it becomes a habit.

=The quality of a person's life is in direct proportion to their commitment to excellence, regardless of their chosen field of endeavor.

Vince Lombardi-NFL

=Leaders aren't born they are made. And they are made just like anything else, through hard work. And that's the price we'll have to pay to achieve that goal, or any goal.

=People who work together will win, whether it be against complex football defenses, or the problems of modern society.

=Practice does not make perfect. Only perfect practice makes perfect.

=Once you agree upon the price you and your family must pay for success, it enables you to ignore the minor hurts, the opponent's pressure, and the temporary failures.

=Perfection is not attainable, but if we chase perfection we can catch excellence.

=Some of us will do our jobs well and some will not, but we will be judged by only one thing-the result.

=Success demands singleness of purpose.

=Teamwork is what the Green Bay Packers were all about. They didn't do it for individual glory. They did it because they loved one another.

=The achievements of an organization are the results of the combined effort of each individual.

=The difference between a successful person and others is not a lack of strength, not a lack of knowledge, but rather a lack of will.

=The greatest accomplishment is not in never falling, but in rising again after you fall.

=The harder you work, the harder it is to surrender.

=The leader can never close the gap between himself and the group. If he does, he is no longer what he must be. He must walk a tightrope between the consent he must win and the control he must exert.

=The measure of who we are is what we do with what we have.

=The price of success is hard work, dedication to the job at hand, and the determination that whether we win or lose, we have applied the best of ourselves to the task at hand.

Vince Lombardi-NFL

=The <u>real glory</u> is being knocked to your knees and then coming back. That's real glory. That's the essence of it.

=There is no room for second place. There is only one place in my game and that is first place. I have finished second twice in my time at Green Bay and I never want to finish second again.

=<u>We didn't lose the game; we just ran out of time.</u>

=We would accomplish many more things if we did not think of them as impossible.

=Winners never quit and quitters never win.

=Winning is habit. Unfortunately, so is losing.

=Winning is <u>not a sometime thing</u>; it's an <u>all the time thing</u>. You don't win once in a while, you don't do things right once in a while, you do them right all the time.

=Winning isn't everything, but the <u>will to win</u> is everything.

Bobby Knight-College Basketball

=I've never predicted anything. All I have ever said is, that we will do the very best we can.

=If I came in to recruit your son, I would tell you, your wife, and your son, that I will be the most demanding coach your son can play for.

=<u>Mental toughness</u> is to physical as four is to one.

=Most people have the will to win, few have the will to <u>prepare to win</u>.

Pat Riley-NBA

=A <u>champion</u> needs a <u>motivation</u> above and beyond winning.

=A particular shot or way of moving the ball can be a player's personal signature, but <u>efficiency of performance</u> is what wins the game for the team.

Pat Riley-NBA

=Being a <u>part of success</u> is more important than being personally indispensable.

=<u>Discipline</u> is not a nasty word.

=Don't let other people tell you what you want.

=Each <u>Warrior</u> wants to leave the mark of his will, his signature, on important acts he touches. This is not the voice of <u>ego</u> but of the <u>human spirit</u>, <u>rising up</u> and <u>declaring</u> that it has something to <u>contribute</u> to the solution of the hardest problems, no matter how <u>vexing</u>!

=Excellence is the gradual result of always striving to do better.

=Giving yourself <u>permission</u> to lose guarantees a loss.

=<u>Great effort</u> springs naturally from <u>great attitude</u>.

=If you have a <u>positive attitude</u> and constantly <u>strive</u> to give your best effort, eventually you will overcome your immediate problems and find you are ready for greater challenges.

=Look for your choices, pick the best one, then go with it.

=People who create 20% of the results will begin believing they deserve 80% of the rewards.

=*The Ten Commandments were not a suggestion.*

=There can only be one <u>state of mind</u> as you approach any profound test; <u>total concentration</u>, a <u>spirit of togetherness</u>, and <u>strength</u>.

=There's always the <u>motivation</u> of <u>wanting</u> to win. Everybody has that. But a <u>champion</u> needs, in his <u>attitude</u>, a motivation <u>above and beyond</u> winning.

=There's no such thing as coulda, shoulda, or woulda. If you shoulda and coulda, you woulda done it.

=About the only problem with success is that it does not teach you how to deal with failure.

Tommy Lasorda-MLB

=I believe managing is like holding a dove in your hand. If you hold it too tightly you kill it, but if you hold it too loosely, you lose it.

=Listen, if you start worrying about the people in the stands, before too long you're up in the stands with them.

=Pressure is a word that is misused in our vocabulary. When you start thinking of pressure, it's because you've started to think of failure.

=The difference between the impossible and the possible lies in a man's determination.

=There are three types of baseball players: those who make it happen, those who watch it happen, and those who wonder what happens.

Bobby Bowden-College Football

=Don't go to the grave with life unused.

=If somebody mistreats you, treat 'em good. That kills 'em.

Joe Paterno-College Football

=Believe deep down in your heart that you're destined to do great things.

=Besides pride, loyalty, discipline, heart, and mind, confidence is the key to all the locks.

=Its the name on the front of the jersey that matters most, not the one on the back.

=Losing a game is heartbreaking. Losing your sense of excellence or worth is a tragedy.

=Success without honor is an unseasoned dish; it will satisfy your hunger, but it won't taste good.

=The minute you think you've got it made, disaster is just around the corner.

Joe Paterno-College Football

=The will to win is important, but the will to prepare is <u>vital</u>.

=When a <u>team</u> <u>outgrows</u> individual performance and learns <u>team confidence</u>, <u>excellence</u> becomes a <u>reality</u>.

=You have to perform at a <u>consistently</u> higher level than others. That's the mark of a true professional.

=You need to play with <u>supreme confidence</u>, or else you'll lose again, and then losing becomes a habit.

Tom Landry-NFL

=A winner <u>never stops trying</u>.

=I don't believe in team motivation. I believe in <u>getting</u> a team <u>prepared</u> so it knows it will have the necessary confidence when it steps on a field and be prepared to play a good game.

=I've learned that something <u>constructive</u> comes from every defeat.

=If you are prepared, you will be <u>confident</u>, and will do the job.

=<u>Leadership</u> is a matter of having people look at you and <u>gain confidence</u>, seeing how you react. If you're in control, they're in control.

=Leadership is getting someone to do what they don't want to do, to <u>achieve</u> what they want to achieve.

=Setting a goal is not the main thing. It is <u>deciding how</u> you will go about achieving it and staying with that plan.

=Today, you have 100% of your life left.

=When you want to win a game, you have to teach. When you lose a game, you have to learn.

Lou Holtz-College and NFL

=A lifetime contract for a coach means if you're ahead in the <u>third quarter</u> and <u>moving the ball</u>, they can't fire you.

=<u>Do right</u>. <u>Do your best</u>. Treat others as you want to be treated.

=Don't be a spectator, don't let life pass you by.

=How you respond to the challenge in the second half will determine what you become after
the game, whether you are a winner or a loser.

=*I can't believe that God put us on this earth to be ordinary.*

=I never learn anything talking. I only <u>learn</u> things when I <u>ask questions</u>.

=I think everyone should <u>experience</u> <u>defeat</u> at least once during their career. You learn a lot from it.

=If what you did yesterday seems big, you haven't done anything today.

=If you burn your neighbor's house down, it doesn't make your house look any better.

=If you try to fight the course, it will beat you.

=If you're bored with life - you don't get up every morning with a burning desire to do things - you don't have enough goals.

=In the successful organization, <u>no detail is too small</u> to escape close attention.

=It's not <u>the load</u> that breaks you down, it's the <u>way you carry it</u>.

=Life is ten percent what happens to you and ninety percent how you <u>respond</u> to it.

=Motivation is simple. You <u>eliminate</u> those who are <u>not motivated</u>.

=No one has ever drowned in sweat.

Don Shula-NFL

=I don't know any other way to lead but <u>by example</u>.

=One thing I never want to be accused of is not working.

=Success is not forever and failure isn't fatal.

=The superior man blames himself. The inferior man blames others.

Jimmy Johnson-NFL

=An objective truth and individual reason are feared above all.
Do you want to be safe and good, or do you want to take a chance and be great?

=The difference between ordinary and extraordinary is that little extra.

=Give people enough <u>guidance</u> to make the decisions you want them to make. Don't tell them what to do, but <u>encourage</u> them to do what is best.

=Military leaders aren't made. They are born. To be a good leader, you have to have something in your <u>character</u> to <u>cause people to</u> follow you.

Woody Hayes-College Football

=A man is always better than he thinks.

=Paralyze <u>resistance</u> with <u>persistence</u>.

Chuck Noll-NFL Coach

=Champions are <u>champions</u> not because they do anything extra ordinary, but because they do <u>ordinary things better</u> than everyone else.

=You can't make a great play unless you do it first in <u>practice</u>.

=Winning and losing are both very <u>temporary</u> things. Having done one or the other, you move ahead. Gloating over a victory or sulking over a loss is a good way to stand still.

=If it's important to you, you will <u>find a way</u>. If not, you will find an excuse.

Tony Dungy-NFL Coach

=Take a moment to think about your answer to this question: Am I prepared to have great success and not get any credit for it?

=It's about the journey-mine and yours-and the lives we can touch, the legacy we can leave, and the world we can change for the better.

=No excuses, no explanations. You don't win on emotion, you win on execution.

=Integrity, the choice between what's convenient and what's right.

=If you carry emotional baggage, the only person it bothers, affects, holds, is you.

=You will never lose emphasizing character over results. Be successful not just in what you do, but in who you are.

=What's important is not the accolades and memories of success, but the way you respond when opportunities are denied.

Pat Summit-Winningest NCAA Girls BB Coach

=The willingness to experiment with change may be the most essential ingredient to success at anything.

=Admit to and make yourself accountable for mistakes. How can you improve if you're never wrong?

=You can't always be the strongest or most talented or most gifted person in the room, but you can be the most competitive.

=Discipline is the only sure way I know to convince people to believe in themselves.

=Attitude is a choice. What you think you can do, whether positive or negative, confident or scared, will most likely happen.

VIII. Presidents-Motivational Quotes

"The one quality which sets one man apart from another—the key which lifts one to every aspiration while others are caught up in the mire of mediocrity—is not talent, formal education, nor intellectual brightness—it is self-discipline.

With self-discipline, all things are possible. Without it, even the simplest goal can seem like the impossible dream."

Theodore Roosevelt

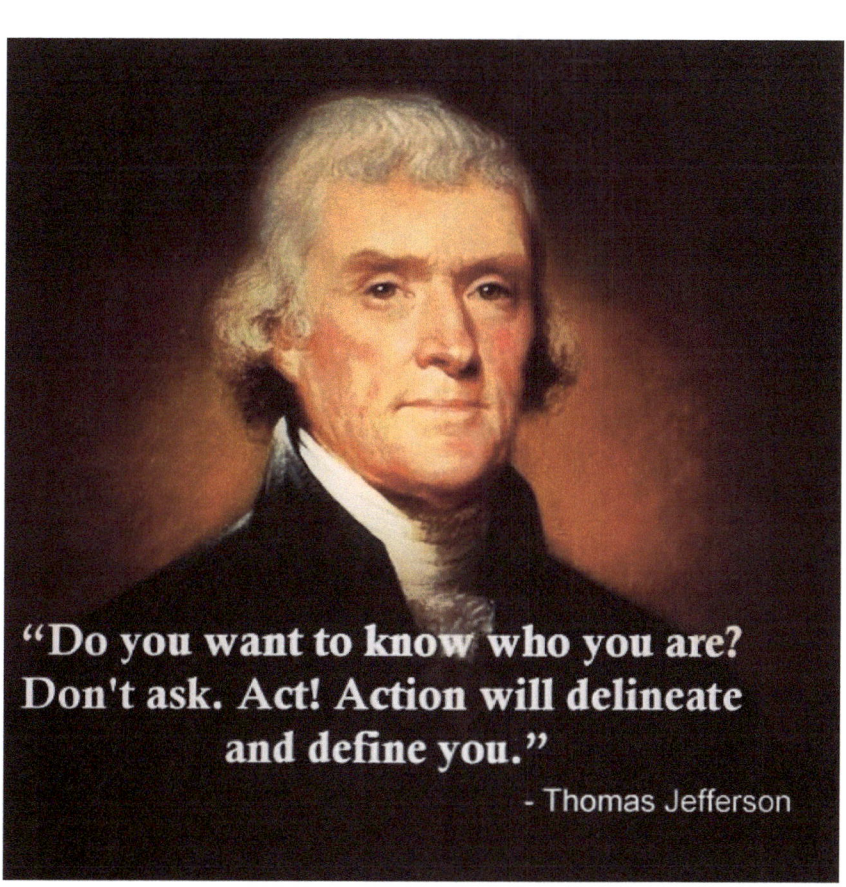

"Do you want to know who you are? Don't ask. Act! Action will delineate and define you."

- Thomas Jefferson

Motivational Presidents' Quotes

Presidents included:

John Adams	James Buchanan	George W. Bush
Jimmy Carter	Grover Cleveland	Calvin Coolidge
Dwight D. Eisenhower	Gerald Ford	Ronald Reagan
Benjamin Harrison	Andrew Jackson	Thomas Jefferson
John F. Kennedy	Abraham Lincoln	James Madison
Richard M. Nixon	Franklin D. Roosevelt	Woodrow Wilson
Theodore Roosevelt	George Washington	Harry S. Truman

George Washington

=<u>Associate</u> with men of good <u>quality</u> if you <u>esteem</u> your own <u>reputation</u>; for it is better to be alone than in bad company.

=I hope I shall <u>possess</u> <u>firmness</u> and <u>virtue</u> enough to maintain what I consider the most <u>enviable</u> of all titles, the <u>character</u> of an <u>honest man</u>.

=Let your heart feel for the <u>afflictions</u> and <u>distress</u> of everyone, and let your hand give in <u>proportion</u> to your <u>purse</u>.

=The foolish and <u>wicked practice</u> of profane cursing and swearing is a vice so mean and low that every person of sense and <u>character</u> <u>detests</u> and <u>despises</u> it.

=We should not look back unless it is to <u>derive</u> useful lessons from past errors, and for the purpose of <u>profiting</u> by <u>dearly</u> <u>bought experience</u>.

James Buchanan

=The test of <u>leadership</u> is not to put <u>greatness</u> into <u>humanity</u>, but to <u>elicit</u> it, for the greatness is already there.

=What is <u>right</u> and what is <u>practicable</u> are two different things.

James Madison

=<u>Knowledge</u> will forever <u>govern</u> ignorance; and a people who mean to be their <u>own governors</u> must <u>arm themselves</u> with the power which knowledge gives.

=The circulation of <u>confidence</u> is better than the <u>circulation</u> of money.

John Quincy Adams

=Courage, patience and perseverance have a magical talisman, before which difficulties disappear and obstacles vanish into air.

=If your actions inspire others to dream more, learn more, do more and become more, you are a leader.

Andrew Jackson

=Any man worth his salt will stick up for what he believes right, but it takes a slightly better man to acknowledge instantly and without reservation that he is in error.

=One man with courage makes a majority.

=Never take counsel of your fears.

Thomas Jefferson

=An enemy generally says and believes what he wishes.

=An injured friend is the bitterest of foes.

=Determine never to be idle. No person will have occasion to complain of the want of time who never loses any. It is wonderful how much may be done if we are always doing.

=Do you want to know who you are? Don't ask. Act! Action will delineate and define you.

=He who knows best knows how little he knows.

=He who knows nothing is closer to the truth than he whose mind is filled with falsehoods and errors.

=Honesty is the first chapter in the book of wisdom.

=I was bold in the pursuit of knowledge, never fearing to follow truth and reason to whatever results they led, and bearding every authority which stood in their way.

Thomas Jefferson

=Books constitute capital. A library book lasts as long as a house, for hundreds of years. It is not, then, an article of mere consumption but fairly of capital, and often in the case of professional men, setting out in life, it is their only capital.

=Never put off till tomorrow what you can do today.

=Never spend your money before you have earned it.

=Nothing can stop the man with the right mental attitude from achieving his goal; nothing on earth can help the man with the wrong mental attitude.

=Nothing gives one person so much advantage over another as to remain always cool and unruffled under all circumstances.

=Our greatest happiness does not depend on the condition of life in which chance has placed us, but is always the result of a good conscience, good health, occupation, and freedom in all just pursuits.

Woodrow Wilson

=I not only use all the brains that I have, but all that I can borrow.

=Absolute identity with one's cause is the first and great condition of successful leadership.

=The only use of an obstacle is to be overcome. All that an obstacle does with brave men is, not to frighten them, but to challenge them.

=You are not here merely to make a living. You are here in order to enable the world to live more amply, with greater vision, with a finer spirit of hope and achievement. You are here to enrich the world, and you impoverish yourself if you forget the errand.

Harry S. Truman

=A pessimist is one who makes difficulties of his opportunities and an optimist is one who makes opportunities of his difficulties.

=Actions are the seed of fate, deeds grow into destiny.

=If you can't stand the heat, get out of the kitchen.

=It is amazing what you can accomplish if you do not care who gets the credit.

=The only things worth learning are the things you learn after you know it all.

=The reward of suffering is experience.

Grover Cleveland

=A truly American sentiment recognizes the dignity of labor and the fact that honor lies in honest toil.

=I would rather the man who presents something for my consideration subject me to a zephyr of truth and a gentle breeze of responsibility rather than blow me down with a curtain of hot wind.

Calvin Coolidge

=All growth depends upon activity. There is no development physically or intellectually without effort, and effort means work.

=Don't expect to build up the weak by pulling down the strong.

=If I had permitted my failures, or what seemed to me at the time a lack of success, to discourage me I cannot see any way in which I would ever have made progress.

=Industry, thrift and self-control are not sought because they create wealth, but because they create character.

=Knowledge comes, but wisdom lingers. It may not be difficult to store up in the mind a vast quantity of face within a comparatively short time, but the ability to form judgments requires the severe discipline of hard work and the tempering heat of experience and maturity.

Calvin Coolidge

=No person was ever honored for what he received. Honor has been the reward for what he gave.

=We cannot do everything at once, but we can do something at once.

Theodore Roosevelt

=Believe you can and you're halfway there.

=Big jobs usually go to the men who prove their ability to outgrow small ones.

=Character, in the long run, is the decisive factor in the life of an individual and of nations alike.

=Courtesy is as much a mark of a gentleman as courage.

=Do what you can, with what you have, where you are.

=Far and away the best prize that life has to offer is the chance to work hard at work worth doing.

=Far better is it to dare mighty things, to win glorious triumphs, even though checkered by failure... than to rank with those poor spirits who neither enjoy nor suffer much, because they live in a gray twilight that knows not victory nor defeat.

=Great thoughts speak only to the thoughtful mind, but great actions speak to all mankind.

=I am a part of everything that I have read.

=I am only an average man but, by George, I work harder at it than the average man.

=I care not what others think of what I do, but I care very much about what I think of what I do! That is character!

=If you could kick the person in the pants responsible for most of your trouble, you wouldn't sit for a month.

=In any moment of decision, the best thing you can do is the right thing, the next best thing is the wrong thing, and the worst thing you can do is nothing.

Theodore Roosevelt

=It is hard to fail, but it is worse never to have tried to succeed.

=Keep your eyes on the stars, and your feet on the ground.

=It behooves every man to remember that the work of the critic is of altogether secondary importance, and that, in the end, progress is accomplished by the man who does things.

=No man is above the law and no man is below it: nor do we ask any man's permission when we ask him to obey it.

=No man is worth his salt who is not ready at all times to risk his well-being, to risk his body, to risk his life, in a great cause.

=Nobody cares how much you know, until they know how much you care.

=Speak softly and carry a big stick; you will go far.

=The boy who is going to make a great man must not make up his mind merely to overcome a thousand obstacles, but to win in spite of a thousand repulses and defeats.

=The human body has two ends on it: one to create with and one to sit on. Sometimes people get their ends reversed. When this happens they need a kick in the seat of the pants.

=The most important single ingredient in the formula of success is knowing how to get along with people.

=The only man who never makes a mistake is the man who never does anything.

=With self-discipline most anything is possible.

=The one thing I want to leave my children is an honorable name.

=There has never yet been a man in our history who led a life of ease whose name is worth remembering.

Benjamin Harrison

=Great lives never go out; they go on.

=The bud of victory is always in the truth.

Abraham Lincoln

=Be sure you put your feet in the right place, then stand firm.

=Character is like a tree and reputation like a shadow. The shadow is what we think of it; the tree is the real thing.

=I destroy my enemies when I make them my friends.

=I do not think much of a man who is not wiser today than he was yesterday.

=I do the very best I know how - the very best I can; and I mean to keep on doing so until the end.

=I don't like that man. I must get to know him better.

=I walk slowly, but I never walk backward.

=In the end, it's not the years in your life that count. It's the life in your years.

=It is better to remain silent and be thought a fool than to open one's mouth and remove all doubt.

=Let not him who is houseless pull down the house of another, but let him work diligently and build one for himself, thus by example assuring that his own shall be safe from violence when built.

=People are just as happy as they make up their minds to be.

=The best thing about the future is that it comes one day at a time.

=You can fool all the people some of the time, and some of the people all the time, but you cannot fool all the people all the time.

=You cannot build character and courage by taking away a man's initiative and independence.

=You cannot escape the responsibility of tomorrow by evading it today.

Franklin D. Roosevelt

=<u>Competition</u> has been shown to be useful up to a certain point and no further, but <u>cooperation</u>, which is the thing we must <u>strive</u> for today, begins where competition leaves off.

=<u>Confidence</u>...thrives on honesty, on honor, on the <u>sacredness</u> of obligations, on <u>faithful protection</u> and on <u>unselfish performance</u>. Without them it cannot live.

=It is common sense to take a method and <u>try it</u>. If it fails, admit it frankly and <u>try another</u>. But above all, <u>try something</u>.

=Men are not <u>prisoners of fate</u>, but only <u>prisoners of</u> their own <u>minds</u>.

Dwight D. Eisenhower

=This world of ours... must avoid becoming a community of dreadful fear and hate, and be, instead, a <u>proud confederation</u> of <u>mutual</u> <u>trust</u> and <u>respect</u>.

=Though <u>force</u> can <u>protect</u> in emergency, only <u>justice</u>, <u>fairness</u>, <u>consideration</u> and <u>cooperation</u> can finally <u>lead</u> men to the <u>dawn of eternal peace</u>.

=Together we must <u>learn how</u> to compose differences, not with arms, but with <u>intellect</u> and <u>decent purpose</u>.

=What counts is not necessarily the size of the dog in the fight - it's the <u>size of the fight</u> in the dog.

=When you are in any contest, you should work as if there were - to the very last minute - a chance to lose it. This is battle, this is politics, this is anything.

=Worry' is a word that I don't allow myself to use.

=A people that values its <u>privileges</u> above its <u>principles</u> soon loses both.

Ronald Reagan

=A people free to choose will always choose peace.

=Above all, we must realize that no arsenal, or no weapon in the arsenals of the world, is so formidable as the will and moral courage of free men and women. It is a weapon our adversaries in today's world do not have.

=All great change in America begins at the dinner table.

=Each generation goes further than the generation preceding it because it stands on the shoulders of that generation. You will have opportunities beyond anything we've ever known.

=Heroes may not be braver than anyone else. They're just braver five minutes longer.

=I know in my heart that man is good. That what is right will always eventually triumph. And there's purpose and worth to each and every life.

=If we ever forget that we are One Nation Under God, then we will be a nation gone under.

=My philosophy of life is that if we make up our mind what we are going to make of our lives, then work hard toward that goal, we never lose - somehow we win out.

=Peace is not absence of conflict, it is the ability to handle conflict by peaceful means.

=There are no constraints on the human mind, no walls around the human spirit, no barriers to our progress except those we ourselves erect.

=There are no easy answers' but there are simple answers. We must have the courage to do what we know is morally right.

=There are no great limits to growth because there are no limits of human intelligence, imagination, and wonder.

=To sit back hoping that someday, some way, someone will make things right is to go on feeding the crocodile, hoping he will eat you last - but eat you he will.

=We will always remember. We will always be proud. We will always be prepared, so we will always be free.

George W. Bush

=Leadership to me means duty, honor, country. It means character, and it means listening from time to time.

=One of my proudest moments is I didn't sell my soul for the sake of popularity.

=Use power to help people. For we are given power not to advance our own purposes nor to make a great show in the world, nor a name. There is but one just use of power and it is to serve people.

Richard M. Nixon

=A man is not finished when he is defeated. He is finished when he quits.

=Always remember that others may hate you but those who hate you don't win unless you hate them. And then you destroy yourself.

=If you take no risks, you will suffer no defeats. But if you take no risks, you win no victories.

=Never let your head hang down. Never give up and sit down and grieve. Find another way. And don't pray when it rains if you don't pray when the sun shines.

=You've got to learn to survive a defeat. That's when you develop character.

=We cannot learn from one another until we stop shouting at one another - until we speak quietly enough so that our words can be heard as well as our voices.

Jimmy Carter

=If you fear making anyone mad, then you ultimately probe for the lowest common denominator of human achievement.

=It's not necessary to fear the prospect of failure but to be determined not to fail.

=You can do what you have to do, and sometimes you can do it even better than you think you can.

John F. Kennedy

=A man may die, nations may rise and fall, but an idea lives on.

=And so, my fellow Americans, ask not what your country can do for you; ask what you can do for your country.

=As we express our gratitude, we must never forget that the highest appreciation is not to utter words, but to live by them.

=Change is the law of life. And those who look only to the past or present are certain to miss the future.

=Conformity is the jailer of freedom and the enemy of growth.

=Efforts and courage are not enough without purpose and direction.

=Leadership and learning are indispensable to each other.

=Let us never negotiate out of fear. But let us never fear to negotiate.

=Peace is a daily, a weekly, a monthly process, gradually changing opinions, slowly eroding old barriers, quietly building new structures.

=The best road to progress is freedom's road.

=The courage of life is often a less dramatic spectacle than the courage of a final moment; but it is no less a magnificent mixture of triumph and tragedy.

=The great enemy of the truth is very often not the lie, deliberate, contrived and dishonest, but the myth, persistent, persuasive and unrealistic.

=The greater our knowledge increases the more our ignorance unfolds.

=Things do not happen. Things are made to happen.

=Those who dare to fail miserably can achieve greatly.

=We must use time as a tool, not as a couch.

Gerald R. Ford

=History and experience tell us that moral progress comes not in comfortable and complacent times, but out of trial and confusion.

=Tell the truth, work hard, and come to dinner on time.

=The pat on the back, the arm around the shoulder, the praise for what was done right and the sympathetic nod for what wasn't are as much a part of golf as life itself.

Lyndon B. Johnson

=Doing what's right isn't the problem. It is knowing what's right.

=Education is not a problem. Education is an opportunity.

=I'd rather give my life than be afraid to give it.

=Peace is a journey of a thousand miles and it must be taken one step at a time.

=Poverty must not be a bar to learning and learning must offer an escape from poverty.

=The noblest search is the search for excellence.

=We have entered an age in which education is not just a luxury permitting some men an advantage over others. It has become a necessity without which a person is defenseless in this complex, industrialized society. We have truly entered the century of the educated man.

=Yesterday is not ours to recover, but tomorrow is ours to win or lose.

IX. Appendix-templates

Student: _____   Date: _____

Theme: _____   ACROSTIC: _____

QUOTE:

_____
_____
_____
_____

Author: _____

Content Objective:

_____
_____

Language Objective:

_____
_____

KEY WORDS: _____   _____

_____   _____

_____   _____

_____   _____

TAKE OVER:

_____
_____
_____

RESPONSE:

_____
_____
_____

Student: _____ Date: _____

Week's Title: _____

QUOTE:

_____
_____
_____
_____
_____
_____

Author(s):

_____
_____

Content Objective:

_____
_____
_____
_____

Language Objective:

_____
_____
_____
_____

KEY WORDS: _____

ACROSTIC

TAKE OVER:

_____
_____
_____
_____
_____
_____
_____
_____

RESPONSE:

_____
_____
_____
_____
_____
_____
_____
_____

QUOTE	TAKE OVER	KEY WORDS/PHRASES	ACROSTIC	AUTHOR
THEME:	THOUGHT OR QUESTION TO PONDER			RESEARCH AT LEAST TWO AUTHORS AND TELL A LITTLE BIT ABOUT HIM/HER

OBJECTIVES	QUOTE	TAKE OVER	KEY WORDS	ACROSTIC	AUTHOR
CONTENT OBJECTIVE: T SWBAT: LANGUAGE OBJ.: TLW:	THEME:	THOUGHT OR QUESTION TO PONDER			RESEARCH AT LEAST TWO AUTHORS OF THE QUOTES AND TELL ME A LITTLE ABOUT HIM OR HER.

SPIRAL Notebook

Directions for your daily quotes...

- ➤ Quote: Copy the quote exactly as is written along with the author.

- ➤ Take Over/Response: Copy the Take Over statement or question. Then Respond in relevance to the question. Think about how this particular quote of the day can guide and have an input with your answers.

- ➤ Key words/phrases: Copy the key words and/or phrases and define them or write down what they mean to you.

- ➤ Acrostic: Copy the acrostic vertically. Use each letter in a word that supports or relates to the acrostic. Ex. TRUST
  - o Truth
  - o Relationship
  - o Understand
  - o Support
  - o Time

  Using Trust as the acrostic, you wouldn't use a word like sly or undermine. Only use supportive words.

- ➤ Authors: Write the authors name down. Research the author and write down a few facts. Why does this person deserve to be the "owner" of the quote? Authors are used more than once. Each time the author is used write down one or two more facts.

X. Bibliography

Today I shall behave, as if this is the day I will be remembered.
– Dr. Seuss

Sometimes you will never know the value of a moment until it becomes a memory.
-- Dr. Seuss

Bibliography

I built my collection of quotes from various places over a span of time. I would write down quotes I heard during shows, read in books, heard on the radio and ones my friends liked too. When I researched for more quotes at home the past few years, the following methods were used.

Web-sites used:

Brainy Quote, https://www.brainyquote.com

Motivational-Inspirational Corner, www.motivational-inspirational-corner.com

Og Mandino-Home, www.ogmandino.com

Zig Ziglar, https://www.ziglar.com

Simple Truths, www.simpletruths.com

Search Engine:

Google, https://www.google.com